W9-CAR-413

The Final Four

43
CLA
11

THE FINAL FOUR

Melissa Larson

First published in the United States of America in 1991 by The Mallard Press
Mallard Press and its accompanying design and logo are trademarks of BDD Promotional Book Company, Inc.

ISBN 0-792-45337-9

Printed in Hong Kong

PICTURE CREDITS
Duane E. Black: 108, 109(both).
Malcolm Emmons: 2, 3, 6(top), 7(top left, bottom), 38-39, 56-57(all three), 71(bottom), 81(both), 82-83(all three), 84-85(all four), 86-87(all four), 89(top right, bottom), 90-91(all three), 92-93(all four), 94-95(all five), 96(bottom left), 98-99(all three), 103(both), 106(top right).
Indiana University, Sports Information Office: 13(both), 36-37(both).
Naismith Memorial Basketball Hall of Fame, The Edward J. and Gena G. Hickox Library: 4-5, 6(bottom), 10, 12, 16, 24(both), 28, 30, 31(top left, bottom), 35(bottom), 41(top left), 45, 47(bottom), 48(top), 49, 58, 64(right), 79(bottom), 80(left), 97.
University of Kansas, Sports Information Office: 1.
University of Oklahoma, Sports Information Office: 20-21(bottom), 21(center), 106(top left), 107.
University of Oregon Archives: 11(top).
University of Wisconsin, Sports Information Office: 14-15(all three).
UPI/Bettmann Newsphotos: 7(top right), 11(bottom), 17(both), 18, 19(both), 21(right), 22-23(both), 25, 26, 27(both), 29, 31(top right), 32-33, 34, 35(top), 40, 41(top right, bottom), 42-43(both), 44, 46, 47(top), 48(bottom), 50-51(all three), 52-53(all four), 54-55(all three), 59(both), 60-61(both), 62-63(both), 64(left), 65(both), 66-67(all three), 68-69(all three), 70, 71(top both), 72-73(both), 74-75(all three), 76-77(all three), 78, 79(top), 80(right), 88-89, 96(top right), 100-101(all three), 102, 104-105(all four), 110-111(all three).

ACKNOWLEDGMENTS
The author and publisher would like to thank the following people who have helped in the preparation of this book: Barbara Thrasher, who edited it; Rita Longabucco, who did the picture research; Adrian Hodgkins, who designed it; and Cynthia Klein, who prepared the index.

Contents

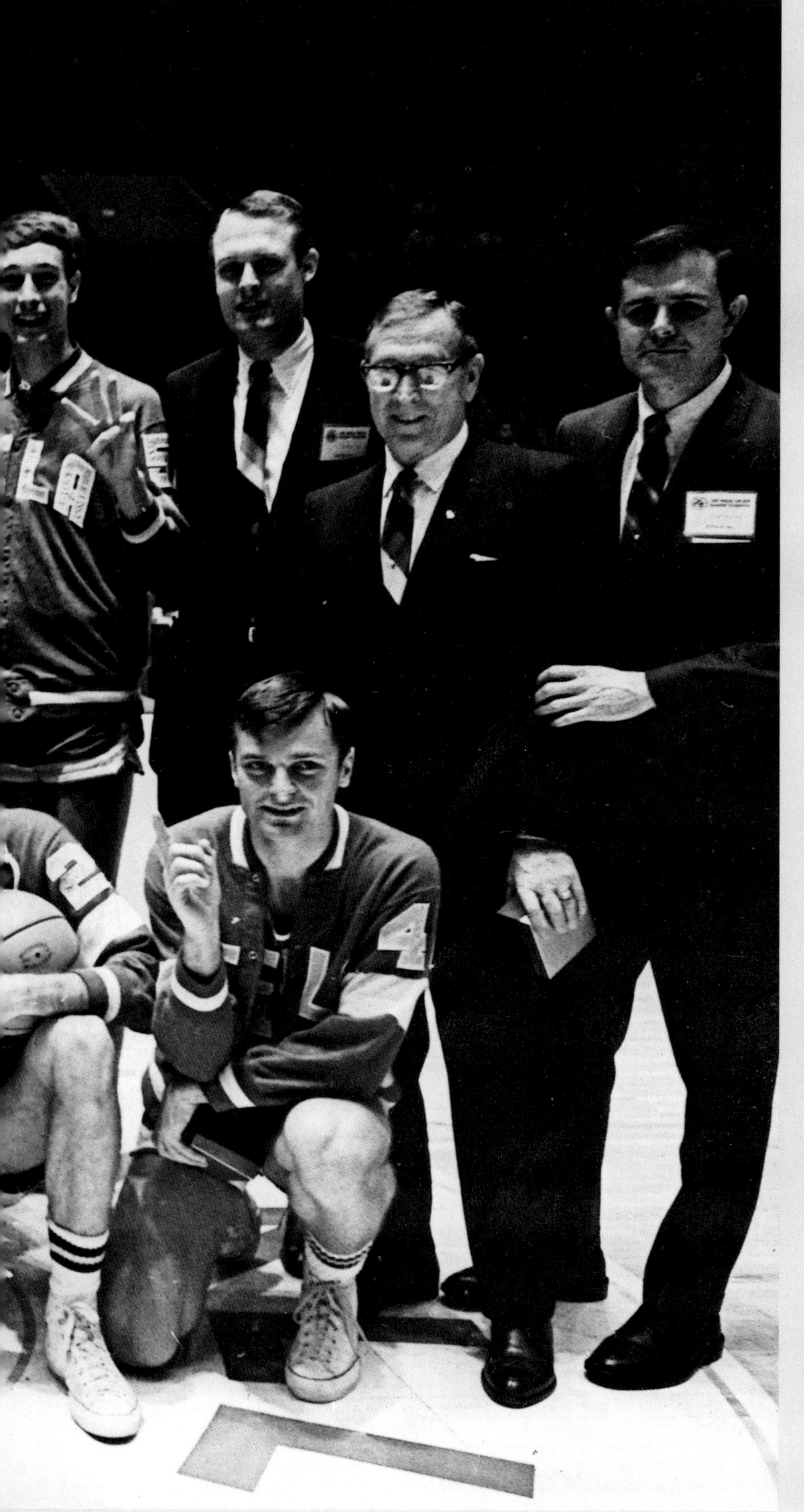

Page 1: *Before Wilt Chamberlain lit up the NBA, he was a star for the Kansas Jayhawks.*

Page 2: *A battle for the rebound takes place during exciting NCAA tournament action between Louisville and UCLA. The sixties and seventies were the UCLA Bruins' Golden Era.*

Page 3: *Marquette gets off a shot against North Carolina defenders in the 1977 NCAA title game. The underdog Marquette Warriors won the championship, leaving Coach Al McGuire weeping with joy on the bench.*

This page: *Classic shot of Lew Alcindor (later Kareem Abdul-Jabbar) and his Bruin teammates on March 21, 1969, celebrating their third NCAA crown under Coach John Wooden.*

INTRODUCTION

America has a seemingly insatiable appetite for college basketball. From a sport that had its beginning as a way to burn up students' excess energy during the cold winter months, when outdoor sports were impractical, the college game has evolved into a passionate pursuit. Lasting from mid-November until early April, the length of the college basketball season still seems barely long enough to contain all the action and excitement.

The National Collegiate Athletic Association (NCAA) Tournament is the crown jewel of this exciting indoor season. Begun in 1939 in response to the popularity of the National Invitational Tournament at Madison Square Garden the previous year, the NCAA Tournament is now a 64-team nationwide extravaganza. Making the Final Four, as the four semifinalists are now called, is the ultimate achievement for college coaches, players and their fans. Each successive year seems to bring a new high in attendance, press coverage, and heart-stopping play.

Today's fans may think the Big East was always the nation's college basketball hotbed. But not too many years ago UCLA's ten-year dynasty under coach John Wooden had experts shaking their heads in wonder. The Atlantic Coast, Big Eight and Big Ten powers have all had their day, and will again.

And don't forget the tiny schools who may one day burst on the scene with effective strategies and brilliant players! Perhaps no other college sport, or tournament, is so full of Cinderella possibilities. While this book highlights only the Final Four participants for each year, the story of the tournament each year could be a book in itself. From fieldhouse gyms to huge, noisy arenas, the NCAA tournament focuses the nation's pent-up energy each spring.

Above: *A Hoosier cheerleader struts her stuff. College basketball has the fans in a frenzy.*

Left: *New York City's Madison Square Garden as it looked in college basketball's early days.*

Above right: *Great coaches like John Wooden, and great team dynasties like his UCLA Bruins, have helped make college basketball famous.*

Above far right: *Indiana's Steve Alford and teammates celebrate their 1987 NCAA crown.*

Right: *Basketball is winter's indoor antidote to the blahs.*

UCLA
54
53
52
32
INDIANA
24
12
Ucla

NCAA Tournament Records

NCAA Tournament Results

Year	Champion (coach)	Score	Runner-up	Third place	Fourth place	Most outstanding player	Site of finals
1939	Oregon (Howard Hobson)	46-33	Ohio State	*Oklahoma	*Villanova	None Selected	Evanston, Ill.
1940	Indiana (Branch McCracken)	50-42	Kansas	*Duquesne	*Southern Cal	Marvin Huffman, Indiana	Kansas City
1941	Wisconsin (Harold Foster)	39-34	Washington St.	*Pittsburgh	*Arkansas	John Kotz, Wisconsin	Kansas City
1942	Stanford (Everett Dean)	53-38	Dartmouth	*Colorado	*Kentucky	Howard Dallmar, Stanford	Kansas City
1943	Wyoming (Everett Shelton)	46-43	Georgetown	*Texas	*DePaul	Ken Sailors, Wyoming	New York City
1944	Utah (Vadal Peterson)	42-40†	Dartmouth	*Iowa State	*Ohio State	Arnold Ferrin, Utah	New York City
1945	Oklahoma State (Henry Iba)	49-45	New York U.	*Arkansas	*Ohio State	Bob Kurland, Oklahoma St.	New York City
1946	Oklahoma State (Henry Iba)	43-40	North Carolina	Ohio State	California	Bob Kurland, Oklahoma St.	New York City
1947	Holy Cross (Alvin Julian)	58-47	Oklahoma	Texas	CCNY	George Kaftan, Holy Cross	New York City
1948	Kentucky (Adolph Rupp)	58-42	Baylor	Holy Cross	Kansas State	Alex Groza, Kentucky	New York City
1949	Kentucky (Adolph Rupp)	46-36	Oklahoma St.	Illinois	Oregon State	Alex Groza, Kentucky	Seattle
1950	CCNY (Nat Holman)	71-68	Bradley	N.C. State	Baylor	Irwin Dambrot, CCNY	New York City
1951	Kentucky (Adolph Rupp)	68-58	Kansas State	Illinois	Oklahoma State	None Selected	Minneapolis
1952	Kansas (Phog Allen)	80-63	St. John's	Illinois	Santa Clara	Clyde Lovellette, Kansas	Seattle
1953	Indiana (Branch McCracken)	69-68	Kansas	Washington	Louisiana State	B.H. Born, Kansas	Kansas City
1954	La Salle (Kenneth Loeffler)	92-76	Bradley	Penn State	Southern Cal	Tom Gola, La Salle	Kansas City
1955	San Francisco (Phil Woolpert)	77-63	La Salle	Colorado	Iowa	Bill Russell, San Francisco	Kansas City
1956	San Francisco (Phil Woolpert)	83-71	Iowa	Temple	SMU	Hal Lear, Temple	Evanston, Ill.
1957	North Carolina (Frank McGuire)	54-53‡	Kansas	San Francisco	Michigan State	Wilt Chamberlain, Kansas	Kansas City
1958	Kentucky (Adolph Rupp)	84-72	Seattle	Temple	Kansas State	Elgin Baylor, Seattle	Louisville, Ky.
1959	California (Pete Newell)	71-70	West Virginia	Cincinnati	Louisville	Jerry West, West Virginia	Louisville, Ky.
1960	Ohio State (Fred Taylor)	75-55	California	Cincinnati	New York U.	Jerry Lucas, Ohio State	San Francisco
1961	Cincinnati (Ed Jucker)	70-65†	Ohio State	St. Joseph's§	Utah	Jerry Lucas, Ohio State	Kansas City
1962	Cincinnati (Ed Jucker)	71-59	Ohio State	Wake Forest	UCLA	Paul Hogue, Cincinnati	Louisville, Ky.
1963	Loyola, Ill. (George Ireland)	60-58†	Cincinnati	Duke	Oregon State	Art Heyman, Duke	Louisville, Ky.
1964	UCLA (John Wooden)	98-83	Duke	Michigan	Kansas State	Walt Hazzard, UCLA	Kansas City
1965	UCLA (John Wooden)	91-80	Michigan	Princeton	Wichita State	Bill Bradley, Princeton	Portland, Ore.
1966	Texas Western (Don Haskins)	72-65	Kentucky	Duke	Utah	Jerry Chambers, Utah	College Park, Md.
1967	UCLA (John Wooden)	79-64	Dayton	Houston	North Carolina	Lew Alcindor, UCLA	Louisville, Ky.
1968	UCLA (John Wooden)	78-55	North Carolina	Ohio State	Houston	Lew Alcindor, UCLA	Los Angeles
1969	UCLA (John Wooden)	92-72	Purdue	Drake	North Carolina	Lew Alcindor, UCLA	Louisville, Ky.
1970	UCLA (John Wooden)	80-69	Jacksonville	New Mexico St.	St. Bonaventure	Sidney Wicks, UCLA	College Park, Md.
1971	UCLA (John Wooden)	68-62	Villanova§	Western Ky.§	Kansas	Howard Porter, Villanova	Houston
1972	UCLA (John Wooden)	81-76	Florida State	North Carolina	Louisville	Bill Walton, UCLA	Los Angeles
1973	UCLA (John Wooden)	87-66	Memphis State	Indiana	Providence	Bill Walton, UCLA	St. Louis
1974	N.C. State (Norm Sloan)	76-64	Marquette	UCLA	Kansas	David Thompson, N.C. State	Greensboro, N.C.
1975	UCLA (John Wooden)	92-85	Kentucky	Louisville	Syracuse	Richard Washington, UCLA	San Diego
1976	Indiana (Bob Knight)	86-68	Michigan	UCLA	Rutgers	Kent Benson, Indiana	Philadelphia
1977	Marquette (Al McGuire)	67-59	North Carolina	Nev.-Las Vegas	UNC Charlotte	Butch Lee, Marquette	Atlanta
1978	Kentucky (Joe Hall)	94-88	Duke	Arkansas	Notre Dame	Jack Givens, Kentucky	St. Louis
1979	Michigan St. (Jud Heathcote)	75-64	Indiana State	DePaul	Penn	Earvin Johnson, Michigan St.	Salt Lake City
1980	Louisville (Denny Crum)	59-54	UCLA	Purdue	Iowa	Darrell Griffith, Louisville	Indianapolis
1981	Indiana (Bob Knight)	63-50	North Carolina	Virginia	Louisiana State	Isiah Thomas, Indiana	Philadelphia
1982	North Carolina (Dean Smith)	63-62	Georgetown	*Houston	*Louisville	James Worthy, N. Carolina	New Orleans
1983	N.C. State (Jim Valvano)	54-52	Houston	*Louisville	*Georgia	Akeem Olajuwon, Houston	Albuquerque, N.M.
1984	Georgetown (John Thompson)	84-75	Houston	*Kentucky	*Virginia	Patrick Ewing, Georgetown	Seattle
1985	Villanova (Rollie Massimino)	66-64	Georgetown	*St. John's	*Memphis State	Ed Pinckney, Villanova	Lexington, Ky.
1986	Louisville (Denny Crum)	72-69	Duke	*Kansas	*Louisiana State	Pervis Ellison, Louisville	Dallas
1987	Indiana (Bob Knight)	74-73	Syracuse	*Nev.-Las Vegas	*Providence	Keith Smart, Indiana	New Orleans
1988	Kansas (Larry Brown)	83-79	Oklahoma	*Arizona	*Duke	Danny Manning, Kansas	Kansas City
1989	Michigan (Steve Fisher)	80-79†	Seton Hall	*Illinois	*Duke	Glen Rice, Michigan	Seattle
1990	Nev.-Las Vegas (Jerry Tarkanian)	103-73	Duke	Georgia Tech	Arkansas	Anderson Hunt (Nev.-LV)	Denver

* *Tied for third position because there was no consolation game.*
† Overtime
§ *Vacated position because players were declared ineligible after the tournament.*
‡ Three overtimes

Tournament History Team Records

Most Tournament Appearances
33, Kentucky, 1942-88
23, UCLA, 1950-87
22, North Caro., 1941-88
22, Notre Dame, 1953-88
19, Louisville 1951-88
19, St. John's (N.Y.), 1951-88
18, Kansas, 1940-88
18, Kansas St., 1948-88
18, Villanova, 1939-88
17, Marquette, 1955-83
17, DePaul 1943-88
17, Indiana, 1940-88

Most Consecutive Tournament Appearances
14, North Caro., 1975-88
13, UCLA, 1967-79
10, Marquette, 1971-80
10, Georgetown, 1979-88
9, Arkansas, 1977-85
9, Kentucky, 1980-88
8, Idaho St., 1953-60
8, Louisville, 1977-84
8, Notre Dame, 1974-81
8, Syracuse, 1973-80

Most Tournament Wins
56, UCLA, 1950-87
55, Kentucky, 1942-88
46, North Caro., 1941-88
37, Indiana, 1940-87
35, Kansas, 1940-88
35, Louisville, 1951-88
30, Villanova, 1939-88
29, Duke, 1955-88
27, Kansas St., 1948-88
26, Houston, 1956-87
25, Marquette, 1955-83
25, Ohio St., 1939-87

Highest Tournament Winning Percentage (minimum 20 games)
76.7% (56-17), UCLA, 1950-87
75.5% (37-12), Indiana, 1940-88
69.0% (29-13), Duke, 1955-88
69.0% (20-9), Cincinnati, 1958-77
66.7% (46-23), North Caro., 1941-88
66.7% (36-18), Kansas, 1940-88
66.7% (24-12), Georgetown, 1943-88
65.4% (17.9), Nev.-Las Vegas, 1975-88
65.2% (15-8), Oklahoma St., 1945-83
64.7% (55-30), Kentucky, 1942-88

Career Tournament Records, Individual

Most Points
358, Elvin Hayes, Houston, 1966-67-68, (13 games)
328, Danny Manning, Kansas, 1985-86-87-88 (16)
324, Oscar Robertson, Cincinnati, 1958-59-60 (10)
304, Lew Alcindor, UCLA 1967-68-69 (12)
303, Bill Bradley, Princeton, 1963-64-65 (9)
289, Austin Carr, Notre Dame, 1969-70-71 (7)
275, Jerry West, West Va., 1958-59-60 (9)
266, Jerry Lucas, Ohio St., 1960-61-62 (12)
260, Reggie Williams, Georgetown, 1984-85-86-87 (17)
256, Patrick Ewing, Georgetown, 1982-83-84-85 (18)
254, Bill Walton, UCLA, 1972-73-74 (12)
237, Sam Perkins, North Caro., 1981-82-83-84 (15)
235, Gail Goodrich, UCLA, 1963-64-65 (10)
234, Marques Johnson, UCLA, 1974-75-76-77 (16)
229, Tom Gola, La Salle, 1954-55 (10)
226, Cazzie Russell, Michigan, 1964-65-66 (9)
226, Akeem Olajuwon, Houston, 1982-83-84 (15)
225, Kenny Walker, Kentucky, 1983-84-85-86 (14)
221, Len Chappell, Wake Forest, 1961-62 (8)
221, Paul Hogue, Cincinnati, 1960-61-62 (12)
219, Jimmy Collins, New Mexico St., 1968-69-70 (11)

Highest Scoring Average
41.3 (289 points in 7 games), Austin Carr, Notre Dame, 1969-70-71
33.7 (333 in 9), Bill Bradley, Princeton, 1963-64-65
32.4 (324 in 10), Oscar Robertson, Cincinnati, 1958-59-60
30.5 (275 in 9), Jerry West, West Va., 1958-59-60
27.6 (221 in 8), Len Chappell, Wake Forest, 1961-62
27.5 (358 in 13), Elvin Hayes, Houston, 1966-67-68
25.3 (304 in 12), Lew Alcindor, UCLA, 1967-68-69
25.1 (226 in 9), Cazzie Russell, Michigan, 1964-65-66
23.8 (214 in 9), Johnny Dawkins, Duke, 1984-85-86
23.5 (235 in 10), Gail Goodrich, UCLA, 1963-64-65

Most Field Goals
152, Elvin Hayes, Houston, 1966-67-68

Most Field Goals Attempted
310, Elvin Hayes, Houston, 1966-67-68

Highest Field-Goal Percentage (minimum 60 FGM)
68.6% (109-159). Bill Walton, UCLA, 1972-74

Most Free Throws
90, Oscar Robertson, Cincinnati, 1958-59-60

Most Free Throws Attempted
119, Lew Alcindor, UCLA, 1967-68-69

Highest Free-Throw Percentage (minimum 50 FTM)
91.7% (88-96), Bill Bradley, Princeton, 1963-64-65

Most Rebounds
222, Elvin Hayes, Houston, 1966-67-68 (13 games)
201, Lew Alcindor, UCLA, 1967-68-69 (12)
197, Jerry Lucas, Ohio St., 1960-61 (12)
159, Bill Walton, UCLA, 1972-73-74 (12)
157, Sam Lacey, New Mexico St., 1968-69-70 (11)
153, Akeem Olajuwon, Houston, 1982-83-84 (15)
144, Patrick Ewing, Georgetown, 1982-83-84-85 (15)
138, Marques Johnson, UCLA, 1974-75-76-77 (16)
135, Ed Pinckney, Villanova, 1982-83-84-85 (14)
131, Curtis Rowe, UCLA, 1969-70-71 (12)
129, Sam Perkins, North Caro., 1981-82-83-84 (15)
127, Mel Counts, Oregon St., 1962-63-64 (9)
118, John Green, Michigan St., 1957-59 (5)
117, Danny Manning, Kansas, 1985-86-87-88 (15)
115, Artis Gilmore, Jacksonville, 1970-71 (6)
113, Ralph Sampson, Virginia, 1981-82-83 (10)
112, Sidney Wicks, UCLA, 1969-70-71 (12)
111, Paul Silas, Creighton, 1962-64 (6)
108, Bill Bradley, Princeton, 1963-64-65 (9)
96, Phil Hubbard, Michigan, 1976-77 (8)

Highest Rebounding Average
19.7 (118 rebounds in 6 games), John Green, Michigan St., 1957-59
19.2 (115 in 6), Artis Gilmore, Jacksonville, 1970-71
18.5 (111 in 6), Paul Silas, Creighton, 1962-64
17.1 (222 in 13), Elvin Hayes, Houston, 1966-67-68
16.8 (231 in 12), Lew Alcindor, UCLA, 1967-68-69
16.4 (197 in 12), Jerry Lucas, Ohio St., 1960-61
14.3 (157 in 11), Sam Lacey, New Mexico St., 1968-69-70
14.1 (127 in 9), Mel Counts, Oregon St., 1962-63-64
13.3 (159 in 12), Bill Walton, UCLA, 1972-73-74
12.0 (108 in 9), Bill Bradley, Princeton, 1963-64-65
12.0 (96 in 8), Phil Hubbard, Michigan, 1976-77

Most Assists
93, Mark Wade, Nevada-Las Vegas, 1986-87

Most Blocked Shots
25, David Robinson, Navy, 1986-87

Most Steals
28, Ricky Grace, Oklahoma, 1987-88

Most Games Played
18, Patrick Ewing, Georgetown, 1982-83-84-85
18, Bill Martin, Georgetown, 1982-83-84-85

Final Four Records for Coaches

Most NCAA Championships
10, John Wooden, UCLA, 1962-75
4, Adolph Rupp, Kentucky, 1942-66
3, Bob Knight, Indiana, 1973-87
2, Denny Crum, Louisville, 1972-86
2, Henry Iba, Oklahoma St., 1945-51
2, Phil Woolpert, San Francisco, 1955-57
2, Ed Jucker, Cincinnati, 1961-63
2, Branch McCracken, Indiana, 1940-53

Most Final Four Appearances
12, John Wooden, UCLA, 1962-75
7, Dean Smith, North Caro., 1967-82
6, Adolph Rupp, Kentucky, 1942-66
6, Dean Smith, North Caro., 1967-82
5, Guy Lewis, Houston, 1967-84
4, Jack Gardner, Kansas, St., 1948-66
4, Henry Iba, Oklahoma St., 1945-51
4, Bob Knight, Indiana, 1973-87
4, Harold Olsen, Ohio St., 1939-46
4, Fred Taylor, Ohio St., 1960-68

Most Consecutive Final Four Appearances
9, John Wooden, UCLA, 1967-75
3, Ed Jucker, Cincinnati, 1961-63
3, Guy Lewis, Houston, 1982-84
3, Harold Olsen, Ohio St., 1944-46
3, Dean Smith, North Caro., 1967-69
3, Fred Taylor, Ohio St., 1960-62
3, Phil Woolpert, San Francisco, 1955-57
2, 15 tied

Most Final Four Wins
21, John Wooden, UCLA, 1962-75
9, Adolph Rupp, Kentucky, 1942-66
7, Bob Knight, Indiana, 1973-87
6, Dean Smith, North Caro., 1967-82
5, Denny Crum, Louisville, 1972-86
5, Henry Iba, Oklahoma St., 1945-51
5, Ed Jucker, Cincinnati, 1961-63
5, Fred Taylor, Ohio St., 1960-68
5, Phil Woolpert, San Francisco, 1955-57
4, Forrest Allen, Kansas, 1940-53
4, John Thompson, Georgetown, 1982-85
4, Branch McCracken, Indiana, 1940-53

1939

The year was 1939. Franklin Delano Roosevelt's America was lifting itself slowly and agonizingly out of the Great Depression, and the spectre of another European war was looming on the horizon, vague and distant but threatening. It was an era during which sports, and their heroes, filled an increasingly important place in America culture. Men, women and children, faced with the daily struggle to survive in the face of widespread unemployment and privation, found diversion and entertainment in the exploits of baseball, football and boxing heroes.

College basketball was already almost 50 years old. From its inception as a competitive indoor winter sport invented by Dr. James Naismith at Springfield College in Massachusetts (and first played with a soccer ball and two peach baskets) the college game had evolved a practical set of rules, and competition had sprung up across the country. The decade of the 1930s alone had seen the institution of the ten-second rule for the offensive players crossing the center line, and the three-second rule for the offense occupying the foul lane. St. John's, Rhode Island State and CCNY were top teams of that era.

Perhaps most important to the future of the game, however, were sportswriter-turned-promoter Ned Irish's "doubleheader" games at New City's Madison Square Garden. Although today's fans take large arenas and big crowds for granted, in the late 1930s the idea of 15,000 fans turning out for an evening of college basketball was a very new idea. Fortunately, it was an instant hit. From poorly-lit gymnasiums in little college towns, college basketball had become big business and a proven crowd pleaser.

The previous year – 1938 – had seen the inception of the National Invitational Tournament, sponsored by the Metropolitan Basketball Writers Association and held at Madison Square Garden–college basketball's showcase building. Six teams were invited to the first event: NYU, Colorado, Long Island University (LIU), Oklahoma A & M, Temple and Bradley. The tournament itself was a rousing success, featuring several close matches and then a dominating Temple win over Colorado, 60-36. Temple thus laid claim to being national champions.

Not to be left behind, the NCAA made plans for an invitational tournament of its own for 1939. The field was not quite as strong as that of the NIT – no unbeaten teams, for instance – but the four semifinalists, whittled down from an initial field of eight teams, promised some exciting basketball.

There was Oregon, with a record of 26-5. The Ducks' front line was a tall group, with a six-foot, eight-inch center in Slim Wintermute, and a pair of six-foot, four-and-a-half-inch forwards in Laddie Gale and John Dick. Oregon's Pacific Northwest heritage was evident in the fans' nickname for the Ducks' front line: The Tall Firs.

Opposing Oregon was Oklahoma, while Ohio State and Villanova of Philadelphia competed in the other matchup. Oregon got by Oklahoma easily, winning 55-37, while Ohio State had no trouble whipping Villa-

Left: Six-foot, four-inch Lauren "Laddie" Gale was a forward on the 1939 Oregon Ducks' front line. Nicknamed "The Tall Firs," the front line also included Slim Wintermute and John Dick.

Left: Big Ten champs Ohio State cruised to an easy win over Villanova, 53-36, to win the Eastern championship and advance to play Oregon in the first title game.

Above: In the old days, the team picture was taken in formal attire. Oregon's 1939 NCAA championship team includes little Bobby Anet (front row, third from left), the hero of the title game.

nova, 53-36. Ohio State had clearly peaked just at the right time (they had managed only a 14-6 record in the regular season) and were headed for a showdown against Oregon in the first-ever NCAA championship game. The historic game was played at the Patton Gym on the campus of Northwestern University in Evanston, Illinois, on March 27, 1939.

As at many such games before and since, an unexpected hero influenced the outcome of the contest. Although fans expected Oregon's Tall Firs to carry the day, the pivotal player turned out to be the Ducks' five-foot, eight-inch guard, Bobby Anet. The plucky back-court man, with electrifying ball-handling, scored 10 points as his on-court leadership sparked the Ducks to a 46-33 NCAA victory. John Dick led the scoring for victorious Oregon with 15 points. The NCAA tournament was off to a successful start.

Ironically, later that year James Naismith died. The inventor of basketball had remained active and a part of the Kansas University faculty until shortly before his death. It must have been a source of great satisfaction for Naismith to have lived long enough to have seen the game he loved surging to nationwide prominence. Naismith was gone, but the game of basketball was poised for greater fame.

1940

The tournament's second year again saw a successful four-way matchup, featuring two schools which would become perennial fixtures in the standings – Indiana and Kansas. It also turned a profit, making $9590. Both schools in the championship game received $750 – just a taste of the riches to come for NCAA finalists.

Indiana had finished second in the Big Ten behind Purdue, despite beating them twice during the regular season. However, when Purdue turned down the fledgling NCAA's invitation, Indiana stepped into the limelight – and has never looked back.

Duquesne and Southern Cal rounded out the Final Four. The Trojans were generally believed to be one of the top teams in the country that season, with a 19-2 record. However, they were edged out by Dr. Forrest "Phog" Allen's Kansas team in the West semifinals, 43-42. Indiana's fast-break offense dispatched Duquesne, meanwhile. It was the second disappointment for Duquesne; they had also played in the NIT final that year, losing to Colorado, 51-40.

The finals were held at Kansas City's Municipal Auditorium, where they would remain until 1943. Although the site was less than an hour away from the Jayhawks' campus, the home crowd could not overcome Coach

Left: *Golden boy Bob Davies was a backcourt wonder for the 1940 Seton Hall Pirates, but his team declined in postseason play that year.*

Right: *McCracken diagrams a play. In the early days almost all scouting was by secondhand verbal reports from sportswriters.*

Above: *Coach Branch McCracken's champion 1940 Indiana Hoosiers. Although they won the NCAA, they weren't considered tops in the country that year.*

Branch McCracken's Indiana team, who prevailed 60-42. For the first time, an outstanding player was named: Indiana's Marv Huffman. He had scored 12 for the Hoosiers and, with teammates Jay McCreary and Bill Menke, was also selected for the first all-tournament team.

Neither Indiana nor Colorado were generally considered to be the best team in the country that year. John "Honey" Russell's Seton Hall Pirates, with backcourt wizard Bob Davies, had won 19 straight games to go undefeated in the regular season. However, for whatever reason, the team had chosen not to enter either postseason tournament. Not until 1989 would the Seton Hall Pirates burst onto the national basketball scene in the NCAA tourney.

1941

While World War II raged in Europe and the Pacific, back home in America it was the year of the underdog NCAA champ. The Big Ten's ninth-place team in 1940, the Wisconsin Badgers, had shoved Indiana aside for the Big Ten title and entered the NCAA tournament with home-court privileges.

Wisconsin's first-round scare came at the hands of Dartmouth, whose All-American star Gus Broberg scored 20 and kept his team ahead until some last-minute free throws by Badger sophomore John Kotz sealed the victory, 51-50. Wisconsin center Gene Englund, also an All-American, contributed 18 points. Wisconsin followed that up with a careful, controlled, 36-30 win over Pittsburgh.

For the third year in a row, a representative of the Big Ten would appear in the NCAA final, which would be held in Kansas City. And tournament officials had taken note of the excitement generated by Wisconsin's home-court crowd. Over 14,000 of them had screamed themselves hoarse, adding an extra measure of satisfaction to the Badger victories.

Experts predicted that Wisconsin Coach Harold "Bud" Foster's methodical offense would be no match for Washington State's fast break. State had already breezed through the Pacific Coast playoffs and had upset the tournament favorite Arkansas Razorbacks and their high-scoring guard Johnny Adams.

Kansas City sophisticates who came to witness the

Below left: *The 1941 NCAA MVP John Kotz scored 12 points in the title game.*

Below: *The victorious 1941 Wisconsin Badger team. The experts considered them too slow and plodding – but superior heart won the day.*

Right: *Wisconsin Coach Bud Foster had his team well-prepared for the title game against Washington State.*

finals must have smiled at the Badgers' striped socks, leather kneepads and plodding style of offense. But once the game began it was evident that Wisconsin was well-prepared. Badger center Englund – although shorter – dominated State's six-foot, seven-inch center Paul Lindeman. Washington State endured a nine-minute scoring drought in the first half and struggled again in the second half. Wisconsin's slow-but-steady attack settled the matter, 39-34, to take the crown. John Kotz scored 12 points in the final game and was rewarded with MVP honors.

Not until 1946 would there evolve a consolation game between the semifinal losers – so Pittsburgh and the Arkansas Razorbacks had to content themselves with getting that far.

1942

With the nation at war, basketball and other college sports were providing a vital antidote to gloomy thoughts. Although the ranks of players were depleted, everyone tried to field a team and keep going.

In the year 1942 it was Stanford's turn for NCAA glory. Coached by Everett Dean, the Stanford Cardinals defeated Ivy League power Dartmouth in the finals, 53-38, on the shooting of MVP Howard Dallmar. Dallmar had assumed the leadership in the final game when a bout with the flu kept star forward Jim Pollard out of the lineup.

Years later Pollard, who went on to stardom and five NBA championships with the Minneapolis Lakers, reminisced with basketball analyst Billy Packer about the illness which kept him out of the biggest college game of his career: 'I missed the final game. I was really crying. I was an 18-year-old sophomore, and I was playing the best ball I had played in my life. I got out of bed one morning with a really bad case of sinus. That was the days before penicillin so I was given sulfa drugs and had a bad reaction to the sulfa. I got out of bed about 7:30 to go to the game on Saturday night at 8:00. I had to bundle up; the doctor was with me. I had to put a towel over my head or he wouldn't let me go. As soon as the game was over I had to go back to the hotel.

"The guy who really came through and won Most Valuable Player was Howie Dallmar. Dallmar was a great ball player, and he just stepped forward. Everett Dean knew how to motivate players. I don't know how he did it, but before the earlier game he had talked to mbe about picking up the scoring slack. Before my big games in the early rounds, I was so excited that I didn't go to sleep until 4:30 the next morning. I think he did the same thing with Howie before the championship."

Colorado, by then a tournament perennial, and Kentucky rounded out the Final Four that year. For Adolph Rupp and his Kentucky Wildcats, it was their first appearance in the tournament – an event they would own for several years of glory.

Stanford celebrated its victory, no doubt never guessing that it would be the school's last appearance in the NCAA Final Four. It went on to greater prominence as a football power, and as a scholastic giant.

Below: *Howard Dallmar (standing fourth from left) with pro basketball's first champs, the BAA Philadelphia Warriors of 1946-7. Dallmar's first moment in the sun occurred in the 1942 tourney, when he shot the game of his life for Stanford and became the tournament MVP.*

1943

In 1943 the war-ravaged tournament final moved to New York City's Madison Square Garden, where it would reside for the next six years. Chicago's DePaul University, with Coach Ray Meyer and interesting six-foot, ten-inch freshman George Mikan, made the Final Four along with Texas, Georgetown and Wyoming. Mikan, one of college basketball's first "big men," would go on to greater glory at DePaul, but that year his team bowed to Georgetown, 53-49.

Several factors had combined to give DePaul its chance to be in the Final Four. First, Mikan was too tall to be drafted into the military, and Meyer was able to build a talented young team around him. Second, school officials at the University of Illinois turned down the invitation of the NCAA for Illinois' Whiz Kids with star Andy Phillip, considered the best team in the nation, to represent the Midwest. DePaul went in their place. Mikan and DePaul would do better in NIT play, but it would be another 36 years before they would be in the NCAA Final Four again.

In the final Georgetown matched up with Wyoming. Coach Everett Shelton's Cowboys had beaten Texas in the Western semifinal, after falling behind early. All-American Texas star John Hargis scored 29 points but got into foul trouble late and let Wyoming slip into the championship game.

After a low-scoring first half Wyoming led in the final, 18-16. Both teams seemed slow and intimidated by the Garden crowd of 13,000. In a seesaw second half Georgetown clung to a five-point lead late in the third quarter. The Cowboys caught them, then put on a scoring clinic in the final 90 seconds of the contest to claim the NCAA championship, 46-34.

Wyoming star Kenny Sailors earned MVP honors, scoring 16 points in the final. However, Texas' Hargis had set an NCAA record with 59 points in his two games. After the tourney, the Red Cross Classic, a war-effort benefit game, pitted Wyoming against NIT champion St. John's. Wyoming won, 52-47, claiming bragging rights for the NCAA.

Above: The 1943 NCAA champions, the University of Wyoming, seen here crowding around Coach Everett Shelton and their trophy after beating St. John's in the Red Cross Classic.

Right: Tourney MVP Cowboy Kenny Sailors, shown here blocking a pass in the 1943 championship game. Sailors scored 16 points in the final.

1944

The 1944 tournament finals saw surprising Utah edge out Dartmouth, 42-40, in the tournament's first overtime. The Utes had lost early in the NIT, but in an ironic twist of fate were chosen to replace Arkansas in the NCAA affair after several members of the Arkansas team were injured in an auto accident. Vadal Peterson's team returned to Madison Square Garden – the site of their NIT loss – for the finals.

But this seemed to be a different Utah team! After topping Iowa State, 40-31, in the West regional, they found themselves facing Dartmouth for the NCAA championship. Dartmouth had beaten Ohio State for the Eastern regional title.

And what a nail biter the title game was. Utah featured freshman star Arnold Ferrin and fine five-foot, seven-inch guard Wat Misaka – a Japanese-American who was short in stature but long on heart. Pesky Dartmouth kept it close in front of a throng of 15,000 fans. Dick McGuire's bank shot at the buzzer tied it for Dartmouth and sent the title game into OT for the first time.

"I remember that Dartmouth's McGuire was running down the left sideline around midcourt and threw the ball in to put it into overtime," recalled Ferrin later. "He was just inside halfcourt. It was a left-handed shot, and he banked it off the board. It was hard to have somebody do that to you when you think you've got the game won."

But Utah wasn't finished yet! As the overtime period began, Peterson's players reached down deep and looked to six-foot, three-inch Ferrin to lead them. And lead them he did, tallying four free throws and making it possible for Herb Wilkinson's one-hander, in the waning seconds, to ice the 42-40 victory. For Ferrin's efforts he took home MVP honors. Utah then capped its comeback story by handily defeating NIT champ St. John's in the Red Cross Classic, 43-36.

About the title game and its aftermath, Ferrin later recalled, "We knew that Dartmouth had accumulated all the good players on the East Coast, or at least a number of them. They had a Navy/Marine program up there. One of the things I remember is that after the tournament there was going to be a Red Cross benefit game between the winner of the NCAA and the winner of the NIT. Before we played Dartmouth, the Dartmouth players told us that their off-campus passes had expired, and if they won the NCAA title, they would not be able to stay off-campus any longer and play in the benefit game. They'd have to go back to school, and we'd have to take their place and play the winner of the NIT as losers. That was a little incentive. How'd you like to stay and play that game as a loser?"

Left: It was trophy time for Coach Vadal Peterson's Utes, after they beat Iowa State for the West regional. The Utes went on to defeat Dartmouth, 42-40, for the 1944 NCAA title.

Right: Utah star Arnie Ferrin passes to little Wat Misaka (21) in the cliffhanger overtime title game against Dartmouth.

Below: Dartmouth earned its title shot by beating a tough Ohio State team, 60-53, in the Eastern regional final. Here Dartmouth's Harry Leggat and Ohio State's Paul Huston go after a loose ball.

1945

With the war drawing to a close and the sport of college basketball on the rise once more, the 1944-45 season featured plenty of excitement.

DePaul's George Mikan and Oklahoma A & M's seven-foot Bob Kurland were proving that the future of the college game belonged to the big men. They clogged the defense, blocking easy shots and changing the tempo of the game with their very physical presence.

Mikan led the nation in scoring that year but DePaul, mindful that the Midwest representative in the NCAA tournament was usually a representative of the Big Ten, elected to accept the NIT's bid.

Mikan's giant counterpart, Bob Kurland, helped bring his school the NCAA championship that year. Oklahoma A & M, coached by Henry Iba, met the NYU Violets in front of a capacity crowd of 18,500 at Madison Square Garden. The fans were in a frenzy over an NCAA championship played on their home turf, which at last featured a New York team.

However, they quieted down considerably after the game began. The NYU Violets played it close and tight, but they were no match for the Aggies and "Foothills" Kurland. He scored 22 points and was awarded MVP honors as Oklahoma A & M earned a 49-45 win.

Then the really big news was that DePaul, aced out of the NCAA tourney by the Big Ten, had won the National Invitation Tournament, and another Red Cross benefit game had been arranged between the NCAA and NIT winners. At last, Kurland and Mikan would go head to head! Another capacity crowd jammed the Garden to see

the two giants who were changing college basketball to fit their own outsized image. Oklahoma won the game, 52-44, although both big men got into foul trouble and neither really played well. However, each had another year of eligibility remaining.

Kurland, who remained an amateur after his college days were over, later reminisced about the excitement and challenge of playing for the NCAA title in those early days: "Our coach, Hank Iba, got the scouting reports, probably from radio announcers or from fellow coaches. Films were very scarce in those days. Many times you would walk on the court and get a surprise that would require a major adjustment. In my opinion, we never had the best athletic material. But what we had was a number of plans and strategies that were applicable against the stars of the games we were playing, and I think in a matter of five minutes Coach Iba could adjust our game plan to any circumstance we ran into. Many times we discovered if the guy was right- or left-handed after he had thrown in two or three . . . We didn't have scouting reports.

Left: *The Aggies triumphant. Note the unusual logos on the team's warmup jackets. Bob Kurland, one of college basketball's first big men, is standing betwen NCAA Commissioner Wilson and Coach Iba.*

Above: *Bob Kurland, the preeminent college star for several seasons, never turned professional. Instead he joined Phillips Petroleum and played for their "66ers" of the AAU.*

Above right: *DePaul's George Mikan, cast as a rival to Bob Kurland, was actually a mild-mannered giant who shunned the spotlight.*

"I first heard of the NCAA tournament in 1944 when we played in the NIT. We had looked hopefully to the NCAA because Henry Iba liked the structure of the tournament. He felt we would feel more comfortable playing in it. We got invited to the NIT that year and got fourth place in it (after losing to Mikan and DePaul in the semifinals). We were aware that the other tournament was going on because Utah had played in the NIT and had been knocked out by Kentucky but had gone on and won the NCAA with Arnie Ferrin. So we were aware there was another tournament, and as we began the NIT, we thought even if we get licked maybe we can get into the NCAA because we had a pretty good club.

"But the NCAA today, compared to what it was then, is entirely different. Today, they talk about millions of dollars. I would estimate if Oklahoma A & M took home few thousand dollars from the NCAA in 1944 it would have been a great benefit to a struggling athletic program."

1946

The 1946 Final Four again saw the Aggies participating, with Kurland the centerpiece of their defensive strategy. Averaging about 19 points a game in Iba's control offense during the regular season, Kurland was turned loose only in the last regular game of the year against St. Louis University – and he electrified his hometown fans by tallying 58 points.

North Carolina, Ohio State and California were the other three teams participating that year. Oklahoma A & M had handily defeated Baylor University in the early round, then trounced California, 52-35, in the semi's. Kurland scored 29 points in that game. Then it was back to the Garden for the title game against North Carolina. The Tar Heels were led by forward John Dillon and a six-foot, six-inch center named Horace "Bones" McKinney.

In defeating Ohio State, 60-57, to gain the finals, McKinney had told reporters after the game, "I had to save some of my strength for Kurland." Indeed, McKinney dogged Kurland for most of the title game, until late in the second half when both men fouled out in quick succession. Rumor had it that McKinney was a "talker": quick with smart remarks and taunts during the action. Kurland would only say, years later, "I don't know what McKinney said. He still talks of the fact that he got his fanny beat, and I take some consolation for that."

At any rate, in the waning seconds of the game the Aggies surged, to win their second straight NCAA title, 43-40. Kurland's 23 points, and his floor leadership, won him the MVP title again.

The DePaul Blue Demons had not accepted the NIT bid that year, so there would be no more exhibition games between Kurland and George Mikan. The two giants graduated that year and left college basketball behind them. But, because of their success, college basketball was poised for explosive growth.

A footnote: starting with the 1946 tournament the NCAA instituted a consolation game for the semifinal losers. The 1946 tourney also heralded the birth of television coverage of the championship game: WCBS-TV broadcast the game in New York City, and the initial viewing audience was estimated to be 500,000 fans!

Below: *Oklahoma A & M wins its second straight title in 1946, defeating North Carolina 43-40. Coach Iba receives the trophy on his team's behalf, as a towering Kurland looks on.*

Right: *Kurland and Tar Heel Horace "Bones" McKinney, one on one. Kurland's team won, but McKinney was reportedly a better talker.*

ROLINA
GIES

1947

With many college players back from the service, and other talented newcomers, the 1946-47 season seemed bright with promise. Arnie Ferrin returned to Utah, John Hargis was back at Texas, and Andy Phillip and Kenny Sailors returned to Illinois and Wyoming respectively.

One of the newer teams on the scene – a little Massachusetts school named Holy Cross – didn't even have its own gymnasium. What they did have was a wily coach named Alvin "Doggie" Julian, and a six-foot, four-inch center named George Kaftan. He was the linchpin of a fast-break offense, and he had that spark of leadership and zest which made up for his relative lack of inches.

Young Bob Cousy was a reserve on the Crusader bench that season as a freshman guard, but he wasn't a factor in the championship season for Holy Cross. The headlines mainly belonged to Kaftan. Holy Cross entered the NCAA tourney with a 24-3 record – despite the fact that they were forced to play all their games either on the road, or in the resounding magnificence of Boston Garden. They were considered the upstart favorites in the East.

Meeting Nat Holman's CCNY club in the semi's at Madison Square Garden, the Crusaders faced down both the opposition and the home crowd to win in a walk, 60-45. Kaftan scored 30. Then it was time to face the University of Oklahoma and crack center Gerry Tucker. The Sooners had beaten Texas in their semifinal and considered themselves a veteran group – Tucker was a 26-year-old returning serviceman.

Legend has it that, during warm-ups before the title game, Tucker remarked to Kaftan, "So you're the 19-year-old hotshot who scored 30 points the other night." To which the cocky Kaftan replied, "Well, they say it's a young man's game, you know."

It was a battle all the way. Oklahoma took a 31-28 lead at halftime, but Holy Cross dogged them in the second half. Neither school could pull away, and the score was 48-45 in favor of Holy Cross with three minutes left. It was then that the Crusaders turned on the afterburners, scoring in a burst which put them over the top, 58-47. They were the first Northeastern school to take the NCAA crown. Kaftan was named MVP, having scored 18 points.

Left: The Holy Cross Crusaders' Bob Cousy as a freshman. He wasn't a factor in the title game that year, however.

Below: The crowd at Madison Square Garden waits for action to begin in the 1947 NCAA title game between Holy Cross and the University of Oklahoma.

Right: Holy Cross' center, the elated George Kaftan, took MVP honors and a ride off the court after the '47 title game.

1948

Coach Adolph "The Baron" Rupp's Kentucky Wildcat teams first made the NCAA finals in 1948. Rupp, a stern disciplinarian of overbearing pride, was teacher and drill instructor in one. He had a crack team that year, built around six-foot, seven-inch center Alex Groza.

Groza was the younger brother of professional football player Lou Groza, and Coach Rupp had recruited him as a skinny high school senior. He had played briefly in a Kentucky uniform before leaving for the service. By the 1947-48 season, Alex had matured into a lightning quick star. Forward Wallace "Wah Wah" Jones was tough and smart. Guard Ralph Beard was swiftly improving as the quarterback, and the formidable Cliff Barker and Ken Rollins rounded out the Fabulous Five, as they were known.

The Wildcats lived and died by their offense. They made a habit of scoring 70 points or more in games – that was in an era when most teams were held in the 50's. A 29-2 regular-season record had been marred only by losses to Notre Dame and Temple. By tournament time, the smart money was betting on a semifinal between Kentucky and defending champ Holy Cross. They got it – and Kentucky got the win. Shutting down emerging Crusader star Bob Cousy, the Wildcats advanced, 60-52.

Baylor had beaten Kansas State for the right to play in the championship game – but they had not counted on anything like Adolph Rupp and the Fabulous Five. Groza tallied 14 points and Beard 12 as Kentucky made it look rather easy – 58-42. Worst of all, in the minds of the rest of the college basketball world, was that MVP Groza and the entire crew would be back the next year!

In the ensuing 1948 Olympics, the Kentucky squad joined forces with Bob Kurland and his Phillips Petroleum amateur squad to form the U.S. basketball team. Groza and Kurland in the same lineup proved too much for the rest of the world, and the team returned home triumphant with the gold medal.

Left: Bob Cousy of Holy Cross competes for a loose ball with Ken Rollins of Kentucky in the '48 NCAA semifinals. The Wildcats won the game, 60-52.

Above: Wildcat center Alex Groza was the 1948 tourney's Most Valuable Player. Here, Commissioner Tug Wilson does the honors.

Right: Pro debut: Former Wildcats Wah Wah Jones, Cliff Barker, Alex Groza and Ralph Beard, start their short-lived pro careers as the Indianapolis Olympians in 1949.

1949

The 1948 season brought new rule developments and new thrills. The new Associated Press poll ranked teams nationally, week by week. And a long overdue rule change allowed coaches to communicate with their players during time-outs.

But at Kentucky, Adolph Rupp was determined to achieve consistency: he wanted his Wildcats to remain at the top of the NCAA heap. In fact, he went a step beyond in his dreams of glory. Rupp dreamed of Kentucky winning both the NIT and NCAA crowns in the same season (the tournaments were scheduled a week apart in those days). As Kentucky sailed through its regular season, losing just one game, they indeed became early favorites to win both.

But something went wrong in the NIT tourney. What should have been a relatively easy game against Loyola of Illinois turned into a shocking 61-56 loss. Rupp later described his players as "flat and dead." Not until about two years later did the coach find out why.

However, things went strictly according to plan in the NCAA tournament for Kentucky. The Wildcats and Alex Groza smashed Illinois in the semifinals, 76-47. They were ready to head to Seattle to face Oklahoma A & M, which under Hank Iba had bested Oregon State in the other semifinal game. Iba's Aggies were a different team from the one he had built around Bob Kurland – but they were still playing his controlled type of offense, and they were still proud and tough.

Kentucky's Groza, however, was on a mission, leading the high-flying Wildcats to a 46-36 triumph and a second straight NCAA title for the Baron. Groza garnered MVP honors again, as he had scored 25 of those 46 points. Joined by teammates Beard and Jones, he was named a first-team All-American by UPI – and the three later formed the nucleus of a new professional team: the Indianapolis Olympians. Alex Groza's future must have seemed bright indeed – but later events would tarnish his glory.

Below: *Coach Adolph "The Baron" Rupp savors his second straight NCAA title with the 1949 Kentucky Wildcats. Later events would tarnish this achievement considerably.*

Right: *Hank Iba's Aggies of Oklahoma A & M tried their best, but couldn't match the Wildcats. Here, Iba reacts to a play.*

1950

In a year which would reverberate throughout college basketball history, Nat Holman's CCNY team did what Rupp's had failed to do. It captured both the NIT and NCAA titles in one year – the one and only time that feat has ever been accomplished.

As a key member of professional basketball's original Celtics, Holman had known how to win, and had become the much-heralded coach at the City College of New York upon his retirement from playing. Yet he failed to see that one of the temptations of the heady Garden atmosphere, the press, the fans, and the adoration was the possibility of gambling and point shaving. As he headed into his most successful season of accomplishment, Nat Holman was riding the edge of a storm.

Holman's squad that year consisted of one senior – six-foot, four-inch Irwin Dambrot – and four sophomores. After winning 13 of its first 15 games, the Beavers had a lackluster second half of the regular season, finishing 17-5. They might not have expected to be invited to either tournament; but the NIT had expanded to 12 teams and the selection committee offered the Beavers the final slot.

CCNY responded by winning the tournament and, perhaps as an afterthought, were invited to the NCAA tourney. After winning close shaves against Ohio State in the early round, and North Carolina State in the semi-final, 78-73, the Beavers ironically looked to a title game against Bradley – the team they had beaten for the NIT title.

The Bradley Braves had beaten Baylor in the semi-final and clearly had revenge on their minds. In a hard-fought first half the lead changed hands several times. CCNY mustered a scoring burst which gave them a half-time lead of 39-32, and Holman must have wondered if his team could pull the rabbit out of the hat a second time.

But the Braves put on the full court press in the closing minutes of the second half, whittling the lead to 69-68. Bradley's Glen Melchiorre stole the basketball and homed in on the basket with visions of glory. But he had reckoned without Irwin Dambrot! Out of nowhere Dambrot blocked the shot. City's Norm Mager scooped up the ball and went all the way upcourt for the clinching layup in front of a throng of ecstatic Madison Square Garden fans. CCNY was sitting on top of the college basketball world.

Yes, it was a glorious time. But then the storm clouds came rolling in.

Above: The 1950 NCAA title game pitted CCNY's Beavers against the Bradley Braves. Here Beaver Ed Warner is fouled by Brave Elmer Behnke. These same two teams had clashed for the NIT title that year.

Left: Coach Nat Holman talks strategy with his 1950 team, who went on to win both the NCAA and NIT titles in the same season.

Above right: Irv Dambrot poses with a basketball. CCNY's MVP, Dambrot blocked a crucial shot in the closing moments of the 1950 NCAA title game.

Right: They didn't wear Air Jordans, but they got the job done anyway: CCNY's Dambrot in 1950 title game action.

1951

Rumors of gambling, point shaving and even throwing college backetball games had been whispered for some time, and during the 1950-51 season the whispers became shouts.

Results of a judicial probe revealed that 86 college games had been fixed between 1947 and 1950, by 32 players at 7 colleges. Kentucky and CCNY were among them, and it was discovered that Kentucky's upset loss to Loyola in the 1949 NIT had been a result of a point shaving attempt gone overboard by Wildcat stars Alex Groza and Ralph Beard. These players, among several others, were banned from the NBA for life by Commissioner Maurice Podoff.

These revelations, as well as various records and transcript alterations at major schools, led to call for reform in college basketball. Unfortunately, the odor of scandal hung over the NCAA tournament that year.

Adolph Rupp's enemies, and there were a few, must have gained some dark satisfaction from the revelations of Kentucky's involvement. Rupp had boasted that gamblers couldn't touch his team, not even two weeks before the scandal reached out to claim some of his greatest players. His arrogance had received a mighty blow.

However, despite his outrage and embarrassment at finding that members of his former team had been cheating, Rupp was still able to put together a winning com-

Coach Adolph Rupp's 1951 Kentucky Wildcats defeated Kansas State, 68-58, to win the NCAA crown, as gambling allegations cast a pall of scandal over college basketball. Rupp is seated to the left in the second row.

bination. The Wildcats beat Kansas State 68-58 in Minneapolis that year, with Illinois and Oklahoma A & M coming in third and fourth, respectively.

The 1951 season was significant for the NCAA tournament as well. From eight invited participants, the tournament was expanded to include 16 teams. Ten conference champions nationwide were entitled to automatic qualification. They were: Big Seven, Big Ten, Border, Eastern (or Ivy League), Missouri Valley, Pacific Coast, Skyline, Southeastern, Southern and Southwest. The other six slots were still by invitation of the selection committee.

The scandal had affected fan interest, and would for a few years to come. The scandal had also put an end to NCAA basketball at Madison Square Garden, which had been its greatest showplace. Fans and officials alike blamed the atmosphere of the Garden for creating a climate where unsavory characters could mix with players. Also, the affair seemed to cast a pall over New York City's basketball fans, and unfortunately some basketball programs at places like Long Island University and NYU – where the game had flourished in younger days – never fully recovered.

But, luckily for the sport, it had entered the Golden Decade, the 1950s. The era of the modern, charismatic player was about to begin.

1952

The early years of the decade saw the rise of talented guards in the college game – not always big men, but fast and flashy. Dick Groat of Duke, at six feet, led the nation in scoring during the 1951-52 season and later went on to become a major-league shortstop for the Pittsburgh Pirates and St. Louis Cardinals.

A pair of five-foot, nine-inch twins were making headlines at Seattle University. Johnny and Eddie O'Brien were backcourt speedsters who made larger opponents feel rooted to the floor. That season, Johnny O'Brien became the first college player to score over 1000 points in a single season.

At tournament time, however, a big man dominated. Clyde Lovellette of the University of Kansas stood six feet, nine inches, and tipped the scales at 270 pounds – a cager in a linebacker's body. Lovellette's inside power reminded fans of George Mikan, but he was also an able one-handed shooter from the outside.

Although Coach Phog Allen's Kansas Jayhawks wound up on top in the NCAA tournament that year, they owed a debt of gratitude to their opponents in the finals, St. John's Redmen. The Redmen had not only upset top-ranked Kentucky, but then had ended second-ranked Illinois' dreams of NCAA glory. Illinois was led by star center Johnny "Red" Kerr, now a well-known college basketball commentator in Chicago.

Phog Allen's Jayhawks has bested TCU, with Lovellette tallying 31, then beat St. Louis. In that game Big Clyde scored 44 – a new NCAA tournament record. The Jayhawks then headed for Seattle to meet St. John's.

Kansas made it look easy in the title game. MVP Lovellette so thoroughly dominated the unheralded Redmen inside that he registered 33 points and 17 rebounds. When it was over, Kansas was the NCAA champ, 80-63. Illinois took third place, followed by Santa Clara.

The 1952 tournament was also the first time that the games were televised regionally. Also, the number of regional tournament sites changed from two to four, with the four winners advancing to the finals – a true Final Four.

Below left: St. John's Ron MacGilvray scores, among swarming Kansas Jayhawk defenders, in the 1952 NCAA title game.

Right: Kansas' giant Clyde Lovellette took MVP honors for his performance against St.John's in the '52 tournament final, when he scored 33 points.

Below: The championship 1952 Kansas Jayhawks demonstrate their dribbling style. Clyde Lovellette is in the center.

1953

The 1952-53 season saw flashy players and enthusiastic fans begin to put the dark memory of the scandals behind them. Johnny O'Brien was still thrilling them at Seattle, but the year's top point scorer in college basketball was six-foot, three-inch Frank Selvy of Furman, who averaged 29.5 points per game and had a high of 63 points in a game against Mercer.

The NCAA tournament champion that year was Coach Branch McCracken's Indiana Hoosiers, who tipped Lovellette-less Kansas, 69-68, in the close-fought title game. Indiana center Bob Schlundt led his team with 30 points and guard Bob Leonard had 12. But tournament MVP honors that year went to a Kansas player – B. H. Born.

The championship game was a tightly-played affair, as both teams slugged it out with barely a basket separating them. The outcome of the game may well have hinged on Born fouling out late in the game. As Lovelette's replacement, Born had scored prolifically and been a sparkplug to the offense.

The score was knotted at 68 with about half a minute left when Kansas had fouled Leonard. Although he made only one of the two shots, Indiana was able to struggle along with the one-point lead until time ran out.

Earlier in the tournament, Washington's Bob Houbregs had broken Lovellette's year-old tourney scoring record with 45 against O'Brien's Seattle. "Little Johnny" had tallied 42 in his team's opener before losing to Washington, the eventual third-place winner. LSU came in fourth on sophomore Bob Petit's great individual play. Clearly, the level of competition was rising all over the country.

The 1953 season may have also been the year that the NCAA tournament began to pull ahead of the NIT as the nation's premiere college basketball competition. The bracket expanded again, from 16 teams to 22. The field would fluctuate between 22 and 24 teams until 1974.

Below: *Big Ten and NCAA champions, the 1953 Indiana Hoosiers – still coached by Branch McCracken. By 1953 the NCAA tourney had become more prestigious than the NIT.*

Right: *Indiana's Don Schlundt (34) muscles his way between Jayhawk defenders in the 1953 title game. The Hoosiers edged Kansas, 69-68 – yet B.H. Born of Kansas was named MVP.*

INDIANA
34
KANSAS
25
KANSAS
24

1954

Individual exploits continued to electrify the fans in 1954. Furman's Frank Selvy, now a senior, averaged 41.7 points per game that season, and topped the season with a stunning 100 points in a single game against Newberry College. It was the first-ever basketball game to be televised in South Carolina – and what a thrill those fans must have gotten!

LaSalle's six-foot, six-inch Tom Gola was another star that season. He had been something special ever since leading his team to an NIT title as a freshman. Now, Coach Ken Loeffler's LaSalle team had its sights set on the NCAA.

However, the early tournament favorite was, again, the Kentucky Wildcats. Rupp's team was undefeated that year, but just before the tournament opened, three of his best players were declared ineligible. Cliff Hagan, Frank Ramsey and Lou Tsiropoulos had all earned enough credits to graduate. So Kentucky pulled out of the tournament and the field was wide open.

And into the void stepped Tom Gola and the LaSalle Explorers. In the opening game against Fordham Gola scored 28. In an 88-81 win against N. C. State he tallied 26 points and 26 rebounds. Next was Navy, with Gola scoring 22 and getting 24 rebounds.

The semifinal game featured Gola settling for only 19 points as LaSalle romped to a 69-54 win over Penn State. At last, La Salle would play in the finals – but with the experienced Bradley Braves as their opponents. The title game, in Kansas City's Municipal Auditorium, would be the first nationally televised championship contest. All eyes were on Kansas City!

Bradley had edged out Southern Cal, 74-72, to win the semifinals, and they hung tight with LaSalle the whole first half, eking out a 43-42 lead going into the locker room. LaSalle's Coach Loeffler decided to make a change – one which altered the course of the game.

Loeffler switched from man-to-man defense into a zone, and his Explorers, led by Gola, took charge in the second half, winning the NCAA championship, 92-76. Gola tallied 19 points in the game and was awarded the MVP prize, to no one's surprise. Penn State wound up in third place that year, with Southern Cal rounding out the top four.

Then came a whole new way to play basketball.

Tom Gola working his magic for LaSalle, against Bradley in the 1954 NCAA title game. The Explorers came away champions, winning 92-76. Gola wound up with 19 points in the game, and was named MVP in a walk.

15
32
53
33

1955

Bill Russell revolutionized the game of college basketball as a six-foot, nine-inch center for the University of San Francisco. Later he would do the same in the pro game.

The fact that, at his high school graduation, no scholarship offers were made to Bill Russell seems almost beyond belief today. Yet, that was the segregated, racially prejudiced state of college basketball in the early 1950s. It was at the urging of an alumnus that Russell received a tryout at San Francisco. Try to imagine what the next few years would have been like if that tryout had not occurred.

Russell's skills were not yet complete as a junior in the 1954-55 season, but he already played the most intimidating defense any one in college basketball had ever seen. His defense-minded coach at San Francisco, Phil Woolpert, knew just how to make the most of Russell's obvious gifts. And, with a first-class guard like K. C. Jones, plus some solid back-up players, the Dons were ready to stand the college basketball world on its ear.

The Dons swept through their regular season, losing only once, to UCLA. Entering the NCAA tournament as heavy favorites, San Francisco scored easy early-round victories over West Texas State and Utah. Bill Russell and the Dons eked out a close one against Oregon, winning by one point. Then it was on to Kansas City.

In the semifinals against Colorado, Russell scored 24 as the Dons beat Colorado, 62-50, to make the final round. Meeting them would be LaSalle – with Tom Gola, ranked third in the nation. LaSalle had gotten by Iowa, 76-73, in the semifinals, and could smell their second straight NCAA title.

It was hyped as a one-on-one battle between Bill Russell and Tom Gola, but Coach Woolpert had another idea – a great idea. He assigned talented K. C. Jones to Gola, leaving Russell the middle of the court as his personal domain. With Jones dogging Gola and Russell working his magic to score 23 points, San Francisco won the NCAA championship, 77-63. Russell wore the MVP laurel, but K. C. Jones had also scored 24 points – holding Tom Gola to just 16. There was a new king of college hoops.

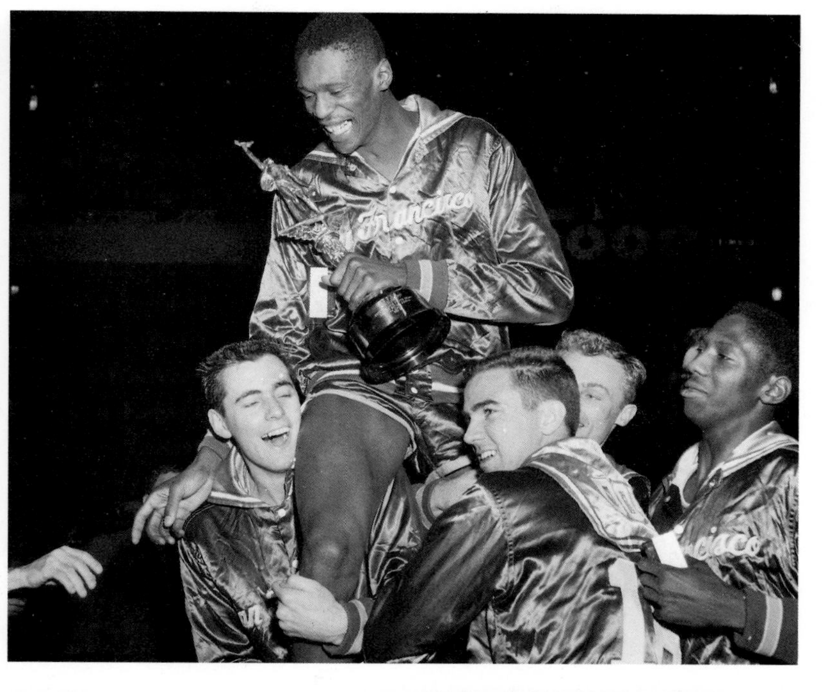

Above left: *Bill Russell of the San Francisco Dons, showing his legendary ability during 1955 NCAA title game action against La Salle. Russell, who was named tournament MVP, changed the way college basketball was played.*

Above: *San Francisco's defense-minded Coach Phil Woolpert quickly built a stellar team around Bill Russell's talents.*

Above right: *Russell gets the star treatment from teammates after another victorious game in 1955. After high school, he had received no scholarship offers.*

Right: *LaSalle's Tom Gola was looking for another NCAA title – instead he encountered Bill Russell. The result: San Francisco 77, LaSalle 63.*

1956

Bill Russell was no longer a secret, but it didn't matter. The rules committee had widened the foul lane from 6 to 12 feet, yet Russell and the Dons rolled on, tallying 25 straight regular season victories as the college basketball world sang Russell's praises. As San Francisco entered the 1956 NCAA tournament, their victory streak stood at 51 games. That lone loss against UCLA the season before had been their last with Russell at center.

Yet the team was not quite complete. K. C. Jones had completed his college eligibility with the end of the regular season, so San Francisco had lost one of the nation's best guards. But with Russell baenging away all over the court, it hardly seemed to matter.

Northwestern University's new arena – McGaw Hall – saw Russell and company brought face-to-face with fourth-ranked Iowa, which featured All-American Carl "Sugar" Cain, for the title game. The Hawkeyes' tourney victims had included Morehead State, Kentucky and Temple, but they were in over their heads against the Dons, who whipped them, 83-71. San Francisco's winner's share from the NCAA that year totaled $12,500.

Bill Russell soon joined the gold-medal 1956 U.S. Olympic team, and then went on to glory with the Boston Celtics. However, he did not win tournament MVP honors that year. That distinction went instead to Temple's Hal Lear, who had scored a record 48 points in the consolation game against Southern Methodist. Temple won that game, to capture third place overall and move SMU to fourth. The semifinal and consolation games were becoming more exciting and attendance was growing. Clearly, the NCAA had a tiger by the tail. But its greatest dynasty, and most storied history, was still ahead.

Right: *All-American Bill Russell was back for the 1956 tourney season with the San Francisco Dons. Later, he would go on to Olympic stardom and a long career with the NBA's Boston Celtics.*

Below: *The 1956 NCAA title game pitted the Dons against the Iowa Hawkeyes and high-flying Carl "Sugar" Cain. San Francisco handled Iowa easily, 83-71.*

1957

The 1957 NCAA tourney featured the largest group of media representatives to date assembled for the finals in Kansas City. Coverage included an 11-station TV network, 64 newspaper writers, and live radio broadcasts on 73 stations in 11 states. And who had they come to see? Wilt Chamberlain of Kansas.

Coach Phog Allen, Kansas' famous link to the old days, was retiring. But before he left, he had won the nationwide recruiting battle for seven-foot, one-inch Wilt Chamberlain of Philadelphia's Overbrook High School. Wilt was in his first year of varsity competition, and people were already saying he was the greatest ever. His size, strength and offensive skills made Kansas an early favorite for the NCAA crown, as the Jayhawks registered just two defeats in the regular season.

But there was a major roadblock ahead, in the form of Coach Frank McGuire's North Carolina team. The Tar Heels had won 27 straight, and though they had no real "stars," they were balanced, strong and deep. In the semifinal matchups North Carolina defeated Michigan State, 74-70, while Kansas had an easier time with San Francisco, 80-56. The two teams prepared for a title match that would go down in the history of the NCAA as one of the best ever.

North Carolina's six-foot, six-inch forward Lenny Rosenbluth led the Tar Heels, but teammates Joe Quigg, Pete Brennan and Tommy Kearns were all hitting shots early. North Carolina jumped to a 19-7 lead, but Kansas

inched back behind Chamberlain, and the halftime score was 29-22 in favor of the Tar Heels. But what a second half it would be!

The Jayhawks played tough in the second period behind Chamberlain's work under the basket, leading by three with ten minutes left. That was when rookie Kansas Coach Dick Harp went into a slowdown strategy. North Carolina's Rosenbluth fouled out with 1:45 left in regulation, but a shot by the Tar Heels' Bob Young made the score 46-46 as time ran out.

There followed two agonizing five-minute overtime periods, during which the two weary teams managed only one basket each. As the tourney's first triple-overtime period began, the score stood at 48-48, and it was time for someone to take charge.

North Carolina leaped to a four-point lead, only to see the Jayhawks tie it again at 52-all. Then Kansas managed a 53-52 lead with just 31 seconds left in the third overtime, and the 10,700 fans at Municipal Auditorium were on their feet. Surely Wilt and the Jayhawks would prevail!

But North Carolina's Joe Quigg was fouled as he tried a shot, then calmly sank both free throws to give his team a wafer-thin one-point lead. In the next insant he blocked an inbounds pass, and the North Carolina Tar Heels were NCAA champs, 54-53. Chamberlain was MVP of the tournament, but would never again appear in the finals. It was time for new heroes.

Left: Tar Heel Lenny Rosenbluth tries his hand at stopping Kansas' Wilt Chamberlain in the 1957 NCAA title game. Chamberlain was MVP, but North Carolina took the NCAA crown in triple-overtime.

Right: Rosenbluth claims his prize after beating Kansas for the '57 NCAA championship. This "no-star" team had won 27 straight games in the regular season.

1958

The 1957-58 season saw a new star rise in what had now become an almost non-stop parade of electrifying college hoop talent. Elgin Baylor of Seattle burst on the scene that season. A six-foot, five-inch forward, he was perhaps the first college player to dazzle simply with his liquid "moves" that faked out defenders. Baylor also regularly seemed to defy gravity as he hung in the air to slam home yet another one.

In 1958 Baylor's Seattle team made it all the way to the NCAA finals, but there they ran into a brick wall in the form of another one of Adolph Rupp's Kentucky squads.

Rupp's team had been ranked highly all season in the AP poll, but the UPI "Coaches' Poll" had pointedly omitted the Wildcats. "I know I have plenty of enemies," the Baron told reporters. "But I'd rather be the most-hated winning coach in the country than the most-popular losing one."

Rupp had begun calling his 1958 unit the "Fiddlin' Five" – a not-very-favorable comparison reference to the Fabulous Five he had coached in 1949. Yet, beginning in the Mideast regional, the Wildcats whipped Miami of Ohio, 94-70, then beat a good Fighting Irish team, 89-56. The basketball world began to take note of some of Kentucky's "Fiddlers," like Vern Hatton and John Cox.

Yet even Kentucky fans agree that it was the "sixth man" – the home-court advantage – that made the difference in the Final Four games. Played at Louisville's Freedom Hall, the championship game featuring Kentucky

Far left: *Seattle's Elgin Baylor began a non-stop parade of college hoop stars. However, Baylor's team fell in the 1958 title game – to the Kentucky Wildcats.*

Above: *"The Baron" does it again: Coach Adolph Rupp and his "Fiddlin' Five" team – the NCAA champion 1958 Kentucky Wildcats.*

Left: *Rupp issuing instructions. "I'd rather be the most-hated winning coach in the country than the most-popular losing one," he said.*

was an excuse for the state's basketball fans to suspend all normal activities for a week and go on a rampage.

The championship game against Elgin Baylor's Seattle team also featured a coaching clinic by Rupp. Seattle's coach, John Castellani, had directed Baylor to guard Wildcat John Crigler, so the Baron simply instructed that the ball should go to Crigler, who drove against Baylor. The great Elgin was called for three personal fouls in the first ten minutes of play. It was the kind of spirit-breaking mind game for which Rupp was famous – and hated. By the middle of the second half, the Seattle Chieftains had run out of ideas.

In the end, Kentucky won the title game, 84-72, as the Baron garnered his fourth NCAA crown. However, Baylor's 25 points and 19 rebounds were enough for him to earn the MVP title. Temple and Kansas State took third and fourth place respectively.

1959

Left: Coach Pete Newell and his championship 1959 University of California Golden Bears.

Below: The two stars of that 1959 season: Jerry West of West Virginia and Oscar Robertson of the University of Cincinnati. They pose here before the All-Star Classic in Madison Square Garden. Neither player ever won an NCAA title.

Right: "The Big O," shown in 1960 as he set a new NCAA scoring mark with 2588 points.

The talent was blooming thick and fast on the college scene in the 1958-59 season. Everyone was talking about two sophomore guards who were rewriting the record books at their schools: Oscar Robertson of the University of Cincinnati, and Jerry West of West Virginia.

The Big O, as Robertson was called, is still sometimes considered the greatest all-around player ever. At six feet, five inches, he led the nation in scoring as a sophomore, with a gaudy 35.1 point average, and was a three-time All-American. Robertson also became the fourth leading all-time scorer in the history of college basketball. But the Big O never tasted the NCAA finals.

Jerry West, a pure guard at six-feet, three-inches, immediately became one of the great clutch players in college history at West Virginia, as he would later electrify the NBA with the Los Angeles Lakers.

The 1959 NCAA tournament featured both Cincinnati and West Virginia in the Final Four. But the Bearcats and Robertson bowed to California in the semifinals, 64-58. Jerry West and West Virginia did better, however, beating Louisville for a shot at the title against California.

But this was to be the year of the Golden Bears. Coach Pete Newell's club was defense-minded and had a crack center in six-foot, ten-inch Darrall Imhoff. They beat West Virginia, 71-70, despite West's clutch shooting and 28 points. Tourney MVP Jerry West went home disappointed from Louisville.

Years later, Newell, who is still considered among the best college coaches ever, reminisced about that 1959 club: "Darrall Imhoff, the center, never lettered in high school. He broke his foot his freshman year at Cal, and I don't think he ever scored in double figures until he was a junior. So he was certainly not predicted to be much of a player his senior year, but he turned out to be a fine player.

"Another of our players was Bill McClintock, a junior college transfer who was a good steady player, but he wasn't flashy and he was kind of overlooked. My gosh, we had really good players because we won the national championship, but they weren't flashy. They complemented each other, they played solid defense, they handled the ball well, but they didn't score enough points to impress the people who pick all-star teams. It was a bunch of players who merged their individual skills into a team effort."

CINCINNATI
12
23
41
21

1960

The turn of a decade brought a new star to national attention: Ohio State's Jerry Lucas. The six-foot, eight-inch center would spark a great Buckeye team, which also included John Havlicek, Larry Siegfried and Mel Nowell. Ohio State would reach the NCAA's final game for the next three years running.

Also an Overbrook High alumnus, Lucas had broken Wilt Chamberlain's all-time scoring mark and had received nearly 150 basketball scholarship offers from around the country. But instead, this straight-A student decided to enter Ohio State on an academic scholarship. And Lucas played smart as well.

An exciting season led up to the NCAA tourney. Oscar Robertson and the Cincinnati Bearcats were 26-1 for the year, and were ranked number one according to the Associated Press poll. They reached the Final Four, along with defending champ California, New York University and Lucas' Buckeyes, coached by Fred Taylor.

The Buckeyes had little trouble with the NYU Violets, whipping them 76-54 as the NYU players fell back before the charging Jerry Lucas. In an upset, however, California and Imhoff defeated Cincinnati and Robertson, winning 77-69 to send the Big O home, defeated once again.

The NCAA title game, as some have been before and since, was almost anticlimactic. The Golden Bears may have dreamed of a repeat, but they were no match for Ohio State. All five Buckeye starters scored in double figures as Ohio State steamrolled to the championship, 75-55, over a stunned California team.

MVP Lucas later joined Oscar Robertson, Jerry West, Darrall Imhoff, Mel Nowell and others on the 1960 U.S. Olympic basketball team which took the gold medal in a romp – many have said it was the best U.S. Olympic hoop team ever.

California Coach Newell, who coached both Jerry

Below left: *Jerry West (center) and his West Virginia teammates take in the sights at Times Square before the 1960 NCAA tournament opens at Madison Square Garden.*

Below: *Fast and furious action in the semifinal on March 18, 1960, as California forward Tandy Gillis hits the deck with Cincinnati's center Paul Hogue (22) right on top of him. California won 77-69, to end Oscar Robertson's title hopes.*

Below right: *Ohio State's Buckeyes beat a tough California team, with plays like this, to take the 1960 NCAA crown, 75-55.*

West and Oscar Robertson in the Olympics, was asked to compare the two talents in their college days: "I think Oscar was probably tougher. Because they are considered two of the best pro guards of all time, a lot of people don't know that they both played forward in college. But Oscar handled the ball more. Oscar played forward more like Larry Bird plays forward. He was such a great passer. He brought the ball up even though he was playing forward. Jerry was more strictly a forward. He was so tough when he got the ball. . . .

"Oscar would go down and get it. Then they'd clear for him, and he'd just take it on his own. There was no way you could stop Oscar one-on-one from penetrating and getting his shot. Later, when Jerry became a guard, he really improved his game and he was like Oscar. You couldn't stop either one of them one-on-one. But, in college, I'd say Oscar was a little harder to defend because of his ability to go out and get the ball."

1961

Everyone expected Ohio State, behind Jerry Lucas, to saunter to another NCAA title. But fate, in the form of the University of Cincinnati, was to intervene. The Bearcats had lost Oscar Robertson, but the talented players who had flocked to Cincinnati for the chance to play with The Big O had formed an excellent team under Coach Ed Jucker.

The 1961 NCAA final pitted these two teams against each other, after semifinal victories over St. Joseph's and Utah. Ohio State was a heavy favorite to win, but the Bearcats played as if they didn't know it was hopeless.

With just one minute remaining, Cincinnati held a slim two-point lead, 61-59. Just then the Buckeyes' Bobby Knight (yes, that Bobby Knight) drove in for a layup to tie the game, sending it spinning into overtime.

In overtime Ohio State's luck, and pluck, ran out. The play of Bearcats Tom Thacker (25 points) and Paul Hogue (22) propelled Cincinnati to a stunning upset victory, 70-65. Jerry Lucas took home 27 points, 12 rebounds and MVP honors – but he undoubtedly would have traded them in an instant for the NCAA title.

Later, Ohio State's John Havlicek commented on what might have gone wrong: "My junior year, we went 30-and-0 until the final game. We didn't have anyone standing in our way. I think we had a couple of games that were pretty close. The final game of the tournament

Left: *Ohio State's Jerry Lucas blocks a Paul Hogue shot in the 1961 NCAA championship game. However, the Cincinnati Bearcats prevailed, 70-65, in a stunning upset.*

Below left: *Ohio State Coach Fred Taylor greets Jerry Lucas as the center comes off the floor, after Lucas scored 33 points and 30 rebounds in the 1961 Mideast finals, leading the Buckeyes to an 87-74 win over Kentucky.*

Right: *Cincinnati prevailed over Ohio State in the tournament, with tough play like this rebound grab by Tom Thacker (25).*

Below: *Later, Thacker hoists the NCAA trophy, as his Bearcat teammates celebrate.*

that year was against Cincinnati in Kansas City. The semifinal game, or consolation game as they used to call it, was between St. Joseph's and Utah.

"As we were about to take the floor, someone tied it up and the game went into overtime. We went back to the locker room. There ended up being four overtimes, and each time we had to retreat from the edge of the floor to the locker room.

"Well, our game with Cincinnati went into overtime too, and I can remember a fellow by the name of Bonham hitting a couple of 20- or 25-footers, the types of shots you normally want people to take in that situation. He drained us, and that was the end of us. I did not have a particularly good scoring game. My role at that time was not as a shooter; most of that was taken care of by Lucas, and Nowell, and Larry Siegfried. A fellow named Bob Wiesenhahn played very well against me. Cincinnati's Paul Hogue was hitting that 15- and 20-footer, which was something he generally didn't do, and by the time we adjusted, the game was in overtime, and they ended up winning by about five points."

A footnote on third-place winner, St. Joseph's – they were later forced to vacate their position when several players were declared ineligible. Meanwhile, Ohio State began plotting its revenge. And a coach named John Wooden went about assembling a team at UCLA.

1962

The 1962 tournament again saw Jerry Lucas and the Buckeyes pitted against Cincinnati, but the game did not go according to plan for Ohio State. For starters, Lucas had been injured in the 84-68 semifinal victory over Wake Forest.

Teammate John Havlicek knew that Lucas was not at his best: "I was rooming with Jerry at that time, and I really didn't know how effective he was going to be. It was one of those things where you couldn't tell what was going to happen until he got on the floor. In those days, you played back-to-back games in the tournament, Friday and Saturday. When we went out on the floor I knew right away he wasn't going to be as effective as usual. I know that I could have taken over more offensively, and it kind of bugs me that I didn't. The night before, in the game against (Wake Forest) when Jerry got hurt, I played well and got 20 points or so."

Meanwhile, Cincinnati had beaten a newcomer to the Final Four in its semifinal game: John Wooden's UCLA Bruins. The Bearcats narrowly escaped the Bruins, but center Paul Hogue had played one of the best games of his life, pulling out 36 points and 19 rebounds to pace Cincinnati to a 72-70 victory over UCLA. "We'll be back," Wooden must have said to himself as the team headed home to California from Louisville. And were they ever!

With Lucas not at his best because of the injury, and Cincinnati's Hogue on a roll, the title game was something of an anticlimax. Paul Hogue's 22 points, and another 19 rebounds, sparked the Cincinnati Bearcats to a 71-59 win over Ohio State, and their second straight NCAA championship. Hogue was MVP and Jerry Lucas, frustrated again, was forced to take it out on his NBA opponents from then on.

Havlicek later expressed his team's disappointment: "The Final Four was what everyone was striving for. And I think it was a lot tougher to get to the Final Four back in those days because you had to win your conference championship or go through some other elimination process, so there were only 28 teams who had a chance to get there. It meant a great deal for us to get there, but it was also very disappointing to lose the last two years after we had won the first one."

Right: *UCLA's Pete Blackman (52) and Wake Forest's Dave Wiedman mix it up in the 1962 NCAA consolation game.*

Far right, above: *Ohio State's Jerry Lucas eludes Cincinnati's Paul Hogue in the 1962 NCAA title game. Unfortunately, the Buckeyes couldn't dodge another NCAA defeat, as they were downed by Cincinnati, 71-59. Hogue was named MVP.*

Far right, below: *Bearcat Coach Ed Jucker is hoisted aloft by his victorious 1962 NCAA champs.*

34

STATE
32

1963

In 1963 the NCAA worked out a contract through 1968 with Sports Network for the tournament championship game to be televised nationally. TV rights totaled $140,000 – peanuts by today's standards, but a lot of money in 1963. Also for the first time, sites for the tournament competition were selected two years in advance. The NCAA tourney was becoming big business.

The Cincinnati Bearcats were favored to take their third consecutive NCAA crown, and as the Bearcats marched into the Final Four, it looked like that dream would come true. Oregon State, Duke and Loyola of Illinois were the other three teams in the Final Four.

The Bearcats had little problem with Oregon State, whipping them 80-46. But there was a surprise in the other semifinal: tiny Loyola, coached by George Ireland, had defeated Duke and its All-Americans Art Heyman and Jeff Mullins. And the Ramblers beat them handily, 94-75.

The Loyola Ramblers had a solid team featuring All-American guard Jerry Harkness, and other fine players Vic Rouse, Les Hunter and John Egan. But they ran into trouble early in the NCAA title game, as Cincinnati ran up a comfortable 45-30 lead in the second half. The Bearcats

Above left: *Loyola's John Egan was a big factor in their upset NCAA title over the reigning Bearcats.*

Left:*Post-game ceremonies honor the surprise 1963 champs, as John Egan steps forward to receive recognition.*

Above: *Rambler Vic Rouse drives for points. It took an overtime, but Loyola bested Cincinnati in the exciting 1963 NCAA final, 60-58.*

were licking their chops. Then the Ramblers turned it up a notch. Their stellar team play kept closing the gap, until, with just seconds left, Cincinnati led by one point, 53-52.

Bearcat Larry Singleton managed only one point on a one-and-one free throw, and Harkness grabbed the rebound. He drove through Cincinnati's defense and scored the tying basket just before time expired.

So it was overtime in the title game again – but this time the Bearcats' OT luck ran out, as the Ramblers' Rouse grabbed a crucial rebound and put it back up for the win.

Cincinnati's reign was over and Loyola was the new champion, 60-58. Art Heyman of Duke took MVP honors for his play in the semifinals, and the college basketball world looked ahead to another season. They didn't know that college hoops had entered the Wooden Era.

John Wooden, coach of the UCLA Bruins, had been an All-American himself, at Purdue in the early 1930s. But it was as a coach and teacher that he would achieve his lasting fame as the "Wizard of Westwood."

The Bruins had made the Final Four in 1962, but it was in 1964 that Wooden's Bruins would begin their 12-year stranglehold on the NCAA title.

The 1964 Bruins featured six-foot, two-inch guard Walt Hazzard of Philadelphia. He had been joined by another quick guard, six-foot, one-inch Gail Goodrich, and a good forward in Keith Erickson. An explosive sixth man, Kenny Washington, helped Wooden's 1964 team reach "critical mass." With no starter over six feet, five inches, Wooden had to devise strategies that would work on taller teams with stronger players.

Bruin star Walt Hazzard later commented on the team spirit that made the '64 Bruins what they were: "The chemistry of that ball club was incredible. First, the architect was Coach Wooden, the philosopher of basketball. He found five players who liked his style, who were extremely competitive and were winners, and accepted their roles with pride.

"My role was the leader, the spirit of the team. I had come from a great basketball tradition in high school in Philadelphia, where I had been a scorer. At UCLA, I became the playmaker and offensive quarterback. I accepted that role. I knew I could have been the leading scorer, but Gail Goodrich was a great scorer. If he missed five in a row, that was no big deal to him. He would just hit the next five. He was a hungry guy who liked to score points. The other players on the team realized that in the fast-break situtations, if he was the guy in the middle, he was gonna take the shot.

"Jack Hirsch, a six-foot, three-inch forward, was our top defender, always assigned to the other team's top scorer. He had the instincts, the tenacity. He knew how to shut a guy down. In junior college he had averaged 38 points a game, but at UCLA he was the defender.

"Fred Slaughter, our six-foot, five-inch center, weighed about 250 pounds. He was ideal for the high-post offense John Wooden ran. Even with that size, he was the high school 100-yard dash champion in Kansas. He played up front on our press, but when the ball crossed halfcourt, he'd still beat everybody back.

"That's what was so brilliant about Coach Wooden. He took the strengths of his individual players and adjusted his system to maximize those abilities."

His plans worked. The Bruins rolled through an undefeated 26-0 regular season, including a memorable win against Cazzie Russell and the Michigan Wolverines.

By the time the NCAA tournament began, the Bruins were marked men. Everyone wanted to knock them off. Their semifinal matchup was with tough Kansas State, and they relied on Keith Erickson's 28 points to post a 90-84 victory and reach the NCAA finals for the first time.

The finals, against perennial power Duke, proved surprising. Wooden's team had little trouble overcoming a taller Blue Devil squad to win their first national title, 98-83. Bruins Goodrich and Washington tallied 27 and 26 points respectively in the title game. Walt Hazzard was named tournament MVP. Michigan and Kansas State ranked third and fourth in the tournament, respectively.

UCLA had its first taste of college basketball glory. They wanted more, and they would get it.

Left: The Bruin team picture from their 1964 championship year gives a hint of the spirit and chemistry which made them number one.

Above: UCLA's Gail Goodrich(25) drives with the ball in a game against Michigan. The 1964 Bruins posted an impressive 26-0 regular season record. In the NCAA title game, Goodrich tallied 27 points.

Right: The title game versus Duke called for intensity and fire. Bruin Jack Hirsch (50) and Blue Devil Buzzy Harrison (34) watch the ball go free as another Bruin player yells toward the sideline. UCLA took the championship, 98-83.

1965

The following season Hazzard was gone, but John Wooden's Bruins had added Edgar Lacey and Mike Lynn, two solid players. They were eager to prove that the previous season's championship had been no fluke.

After a season-opening upset by Illinois, UCLA went 24 for 25, serving notice that they planned to vigorously defend their title.

Wooden's Bruins now shook out like this: Gail Goodrich was playmaker, Doug McIntosh played center, Fred Goss at the other guard position, sophomores Lacey and Lynn at forwards, and Washington as sixth man. They quickly found a tempo of their own.

The Final Four that year also featured Princeton, with All-American Bill Bradley, Wichita State and mighty Michigan, with All-American sensation Cazzie Russell. UCLA pounded Wichita State, 108-89, on a splendid effort by Gail Goodrich (28 points) and Lacey (24).

Meanwhile, despite Bill Bradley's 29 points for the Tigers, Michigan crushed Princeton, 93-76, earning the right to meet the Bruins in the NCAA title game. Portland, Oregon's Memorial Coliseum was the site of the finals, and more than 13,000 fans turned out to see the action.

They saw the Bruins run the Wolverines into the floor in the title game. Goodrich belted out 42 points as UCLA bounded to a 91-80 win. Caz Russell showed class in a losing effort with 28 points. That year's consolation game also proved highly entertaining – featuring Princeton topping Wichita State, 118-82. Rhodes scholar and tournament MVP Bill Bradley set the Coliseum ablaze with a stunning 58 points, before going on to the New York Knicks, and eventually to the U.S. Senate.

For the Bruins, it was two titles down – and eight more still to go!

Below: *The great Cazzie Russell of the Michgan Wolverines gets around UCLA's Kenny Washington in the 1965 title game. All-American Russell tallied 28 in a losing cause, for the Wolverines were bested, 91-80.*

Right: *Tourney MVP that year was Princeton's Bill Bradley (42), who would go on to a Rhodes scholarship, the New York Knicks, and the Senate. Here he gets off a shot in the semifinal against Wichita State.*

PRINCETON
42
20
4

1966

Not content with back-to-back NCAA titles, John Wooden was making plans which he hoped would leave the rest of the college basketball pack behind in their dust. In the fall of 1965 he had succeeded in recruiting a seven-foot, two-inch high school star by the name of Lew Alcindor, and it didn't take long for Alcindor to make his new coach proud. Leading the Bruin freshman squad against the UCLA varsity, Lew and his new teammates whipped the upperclassmen easily, 75-60.

But it wasn't just that Alcindor was so good – the Bruin varsity was simply not great that year. In fact, the 1966 NCAA tournament went by the unofficial name of "The Last Chance Tournament." Everyone knew Alcindor would give UCLA a huge boost the following season, so it was time for other schools to try for a championship while it was still a possibility. Perhaps no other college freshman has so influenced college basketball before he even put on a varsity uniform.

Kentucky was back in the Final Four fray that year. The squad was dubbed "Rupp's Runts," because none of the starters was over six-feet, five inches. Still, it was a Rupp team: strong, deep and scrappy, featuring guards Louis Dampier and Pat Riley (yes, that Pat Riley).

Joining Kentucky were Duke, Texas Western (now called Texas El-Paso, or UTEP for short) and Utah. Duke had stellar guard Bob Verga and forward Jack Marin. The Miners of Texas Western featured no superplayers, but solid team guys like David Lattin, Bobby Joe Hill, Willie Worsley, Neville Shed, Willie Cager and Orsten Artis.

Kentucky's speed allowed it to get by pesky Duke, 83-79. The Miners had less trouble with the Utes, playing at their peak and coming away with an 85-78 win. Now it would be Kentucky against Texas Western in the "Last

Below left: *Bobby Joe Hill of Texas Western dribbles past Kentucky's Tommy Kron in the "Last Chance" NCAA final game. Texas Western prevailed* 72-65.

Below: *Texas Western celebrates its NCAA title over Adolph Rupp's Kentucky Wildcats. TWU Coach Don Haskins (second from left) shakes hands with assistant Moe Iba. "Rupp's Runts," runners-up, featured a guard named Pat Riley.*

Chance" finals, to be held in College Park, Maryland's Cole Fieldhouse.

Rupp and Kentucky were sentimental favorites, since "The Baron" was going for his fifth title. However, the Miners proved too powerful for the Wildcats, leading all the way and prevailing, 72-65.

Bobby Joe Hill led with 20 points, although the tourney MVP was Utah's Jerry Chambers. He had scored 143 points in four games, but the Utes had lost in the semifinals, and again in the consolation game to Duke.

A footnote: In 1966 the net income for the entire NCAA tourney exceeded $500,000 for the first time. But most fans knew the next few years would be unlike any that had gone before it. So, while Texas Western savored its victory, the college hoops universe braced for the coming of Lew Alcindor and the return of the UCLA Bruins.

1967

Left: *UCLA trounced the University of Houston in a semifinal matchup which featured Lew Alcindor (33) against Houston's Elvin Hayes (44).*

Above: *The "Wizard of Westwood" signals for a time-out.*

Lew Alcindor had measured six-feet, four-inches tall as an 11-year-old boy, and he must have been accustomed to his special skills. He may not even have wondered if he was really as good as everyone said he was. But he still managed to stun the basketball world when, in his first varsity game for UCLA, he scored a team-record 56 points against Southern Cal in a 105-90 victory!

It's been postulated that Alcindor could have attended any one of a number of schools and brought them three NCAA championships. Yet, it was obvious from the beginning that in Wooden Alcindor had found a coach who appreciated his talent and was able and willing to mold a team around it.

For instance, Wooden had Alcindor spend much of his freshman year working with six-foot, eight-inch graduate student Jay Carty, to develop a presence around the basket. By the time Alcindor's freshman team was through feasting on their helpless opponents, Lew was ready for varsity competition.

Joining Alcindor on the Bruin team in 1966-67 was junior Mike Warren, a quick six-footer at guard. Six-foot, three-inch Lucius Allen, six-foot, seven-inch forward Lynn Shackelford and six-foot, four-inch Ken Heitz – rounded out the starting squad for John Wooden. This youthful juggernaut of a team rolled to an undefeated season, behind Alcindor's average of 29 points per game, and record 66.7 percent shooting accuracy.

Those who had hoped UCLA would stumble in the NCAA tournament were sadly mistaken – the Bruins embarrassed the University of Houston and its star forward, Elvin Hayes, 73-58 in the semifinal. Then they coasted to an easy victory over upstart Dayton, 79-64, to officially return to the top of the hoop heap with an NCAA title. And the whole college basketball world knew that the entire starting lineup would be back the following season!

Houston and North Carolina wound up third and fourth respectively. And the MVP of the tournament, to the surprise of no one, was the "Big Guy" to end all big guys – Lew Alcindor.

Later in his career, the great Wooden was asked to compare Alcindor, by then called Kareem Abdul-Jabbar, and his star of the early seventies, Bill Walton: "Kareem, of course, was the best performer of them all, and I think he is quite possibly the most valuable college player who ever played. Most valuable. That doesn't necessarily mean the same thing as saying he is the best player. But I believe he caused opponents more problems at each end of the court than any other center I know of. Bill probably was a better basketball player than Kareem. He passed a little better, not that Kareem was a bad passer, and I would say that Bill could probably shoot a little better. But he still wasn't that tremendous threat in there. Bill could rebound and initiate the fast break with the outlet pass better than anybody I have ever coached. Overall, I would say our set offense might have been better with Walton because we had people to fill all the roles. But our overall game was probably a little bit stronger in the Jabbar era just because I think he is tremendously valuable."

Above left: *Dayton's Don May (21) strips the ball from North Carolina players Rusty Clark (43) and Bob Lewis (22) in the NCAA semifinal. Dayton won, earning the right to be punished by the Bruins in the final – 79-64.*

Left: *Lew Alcindor towers over teammates as the Bruins celebrate yet another title. Alcindor won the first of three consecutive MVP awards.*

1968

In 1967-68 a new rule against dunking was instituted. Some say it was meant to try to neutralize Alcindor, but all it accomplished was to make the games duller. At any rate, a few years later dunking was back by popular demand.

The Bruins were jammed with talent for the 1967-68 season, as Lacey and Lynn returned from a year's absence. Wooden switched to a high-post/low-post offense that required adjustment, with Lynn and Lacey alternating at high-post.

Coach Wooden had by now developed a routine for preparing his players and his team for the postseason tourney: "At the beginning of the season, from the fifteenth of October to the first of December, I was trying to get our team in shape and trying to analyze personnel and find combinations that could work. By January, when conference play began, I wanted to know who the top seven players were and what combinations I was going to use. If we won the conference championship early enough, I slowed the team down to keep them fresh for the NCAA. Had I coached in the ACC, I wouldn't have coached the same. . . . There would be some things against certain opponents in a regular season game that I wouldn't do – I might have been saving something for the ACC tournament."

Far left: *The Bruins' Lew Alcindor and Elvin Hayes of Houston again tie it on in the 1968 NCAA semifinal. Houston had beaten the Bruins in the regular season that year, but they were crushed in the semifinal, 101-69.*

Below left: *Alcindor and Ken Heitz (22) block Houston's Ken Spain in the semifinal.*

Right: *Ohio State pulled an upset victory over Houston in the 1968 consolation game. Here, Elvin Hayes grabs a rebound. After UCLA, everyone else was playing for second place.*

The Bruins lost one regular season game that year to Houston, in front of an enormous crowd at the Astrodome. Alcindor had been hampered by a scratched eye, and Houston's Elvin Hayes ran wild, scoring 39 points as the Cougars eked out a 71-69 victory against the nation's number one team.

However, UCLA got its sweet revenge in the NCAA Final Four that same year, crushing Houston in the semifinals, 101-69, as Alcindor scored 19 and posted 18 rebounds. Then the Bruin squad proceeded to undress N. C. in the finals, 78-55, for yet another national title.

Ohio State and Houston took home third and fourth place honors in the tournament, and Alcindor was voted MVP once again, in front of his adopted hometown crowd at Los Angeles' Sports Arena.

Would this team ever lose again?

1969

In the 1968-69 season the NCAA altered the Friday-through-Saturday format for the semifinals and final, extending the schedule to Thursday-through-Saturday. Also, the NCAA selected NBC to televise the championship, for a rights payment of $547,000 – exceeding $500,000 for the first time. The 1969 tournament's net income of $1,032,915 was also the first time it had broken the million-dollar mark.

But if the format and TV arrangements of the tourney were undergoing change, the identity of the dominant team certainly wasn't.

John Wooden's Bruins had lost their starting backcourt of Mike Warren and Lucius Allen, yet barely broke stride as they put together another stunning season, losing only once in an upset to Southern Cal.

In Alcindor's last NCAA tournament, the UCLA Bruins played up to his level as a team, trouncing Purdue, 92-72, in the finals for their third consecutive championship, and fifth in six seasons.

Purdue, Drake and North Carolina filled out UCLA's Final Four hit list that year, but Alcindor's 37 points and 20 rebounds in the title game – his last as a Bruin – garnered him an unprecedented third MVP title.

He had fulfilled every expectation that had been made of him, and then some. He would go on to a brilliant pro career as Kareem Abdul-Jabbar, but will always be remembered by UCLA fans as Lew Alcindor, the complete team player.

Below: *Purdue was UCLA's victim in the the 1969 NCAA title game. The final score in Alcindor's last game: 92-72. Alcindor earned an unprecendented third MVP title.*

Right: *Drake Coach Maurice John gets excited during semifinal play. UCLA edged Drake, 85-82.*

Far right: *Wooden called Alcindor his best player ever.*

As Coach Wooden said goodbye to his greatest player, he reminisced about recruiting the sensitive high school boy who became Kareem Abdul-Jabbar: "His high school coach called me after his junior year and said, 'Coach, you're speaking in Valley Forge, Pennsylvania, in April. I'd like to come and talk to you about my player, Alcindor. You'll be pleased about what I have to say.' He went on to tell me that Jabbar was going to visit five schools his senior year and that UCLA was one of his picks. . . . At the conclusion of [Alcindor's] 48-hour visit, he said, 'I'm coming to UCLA.' Then, to show you what kind of individual he is, sometime later he called me and asked me if I would come and visit his folks. He said his parents would like to meet the coach for whom he was going to play . . . . So Jerry [Norman] and I took the trip, and we met Kareem's parents at one o'clock in the morning because his father was working the noon-to-midnight shift."

The question before the rest of college basketball was, could Wooden and the Bruins win without Lew Alcindor?

3

1970

In the early 1969-70 season the Bruins' opponents were feeling hopeful. John Wooden had not recruited a star center to replace Lew Alcindor, so it seemed just possible that UCLA might be just another good team that year. But Coach Wooden was about to prove that he could win without big stars, as well as he could win with them.

Steve Patterson, a six-foot, nine-inch player, was moved to center. Patterson was highly coachable and mobile. Wooden's forwards that year were outstanding: six-foot, seven-inch junior Curtis Rowe, and six-foot, nine-inch sophomore Sidney Wicks. He also boasted both a shooting guard in John Vallely and a quick point guard, sharpshooter Henry Bibby.

To most fans' astonishment, this solid and unselfish group of players kept the Bruin dynasty rolling, compiling a 24-2 regular season record.

"This team gave me as much satisfaction as any team I coached," Wooden said, in assessing his team's chances for a fourth straight NCAA title. "We had a lot of close games, but they would always find a way to pull them out."

Other teams making it to the Final Four that year were surprising Jacksonville, with its seven-foot, two-inch center Artis Gilmore, New Mexico State and St. Bonaventure. Unfortunately, St. Bonaventure's six-foot, eleven-inch star Big Bob Lanier had injured his knee in the East final against Villanova, and needed surgery. Without him, St. Bonaventure bowed easily before Jacksonville.

UCLA had a relatively easy time, beating New Mexico, 93-77, in the semifinals. But how would they fare against Jacksonville's Gilmore and seven-footer Pembrook Burrows?

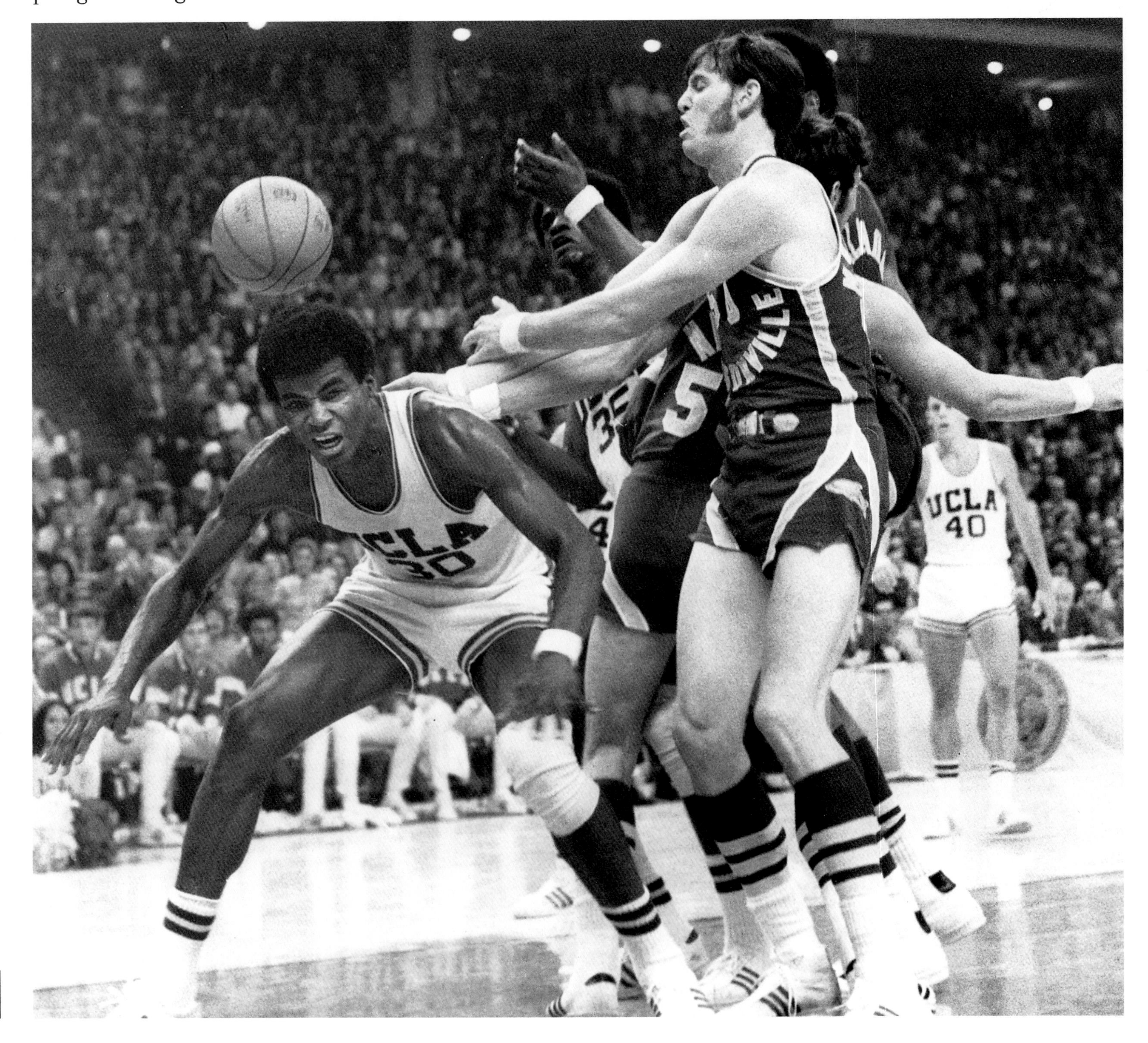

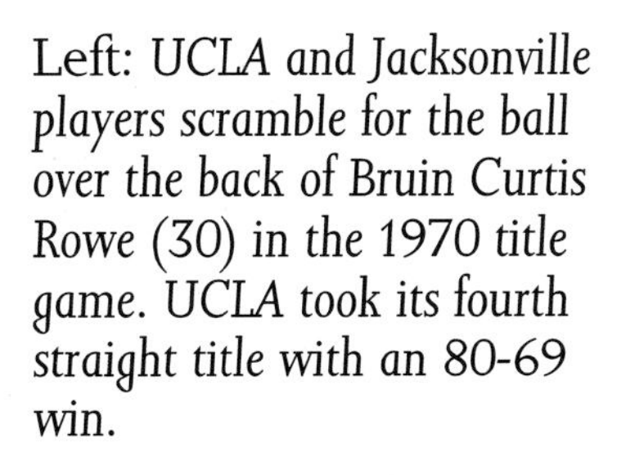
Left: UCLA and Jacksonville players scramble for the ball over the back of Bruin Curtis Rowe (30) in the 1970 title game. UCLA took its fourth straight title with an 80-69 win.

Above: Sidney Wicks (35) hauls in a rebound as the finals action continues fast and furious. At right is Jacksonville's goatee'd Artis Gilmore.

Above right: UCLA's Henry Bibby (45) bags a layup in the big game. Wooden's Bruins were proving they could win championships without Alcindor.

Right: Artis Gilmore (left) was the tallest man on the court at seven feet two inches, but UCLA's Sidney Wicks (35) neutralized him.

As usual, Wooden had a plan. He assigned Wicks to Gilmore, and the smaller player's speed and agility denied the goatee'd Gilmore many scoring opportunities. The Bruins' overall consistent play earned them an 80-69 win and yet another championship.

Wicks' 17 points and 18 rebounds, as well as his sterling defensive performance, garnered him MVP honors. But it was teammate Curtis Rowe who summed up the team's pride when he said, "For three years, everybody always said Lew did it. Well, we just proved that four other men from that team could play basketball."

1971

The Bruin juggernaut rolled on. Only one regular season loss marred their brilliance – to Notre Dame and Austin Carr's 46-point individual performance. Come NCAA tournament time, they were ready to go again, but it wouldn't be easy.

Against regional final opponent Long Beach State, UCLA received quite a scare as they managed to win by only two points, 57-55.

The Final Four went a little more according to the script for the Bruins. Beating Kansas in the semifinals, 68-60, UCLA moved on to the final against Villanova and six-foot, eight-inch All-American Howard Porter.

If it had not been for the brilliant play of center Steve Patterson, there might have been a stunning upset. Patterson scored 29 as the grateful Bruins eked out another NCAA title, beating the Villanova Wildcats, 68-62. Villanova's Howard Porter received MVP honors for the runners-up, and Western Kentucky and Kansas wound up in third and fourth place, respectively. However, players for both Villanova and Western Kentucky were later declared ineligible, so the Final Four records for 1971 are marked with asterisks.

A tournament footnote: NBC recorded the largest audience ever for a basketball network telecast during the semifinals, as an estimated 9,320,000 homes received the game.

Coach John Wooden would now have to struggle on without his entire front line of Wicks, Rowe and Patterson. However, at a press conference shortly after the tournament, Wooden announced he had found a new center for his 1972 UCLA Bruins: a redheaded kid named Bill Walton.

"Bill had an older brother, Bruce, who was on our football team," Wooden later recalled. "He was two years ahead of Bill, but Bill had come to football games with his parents. I had met Bill earlier. He was one of the few players outside the greater Los Angeles area that I went to watch play in high school and one of the few players I ever visited in his home. I thought from the very beginning he was going to come to UCLA."

Left: Semifinal play featured Villanova and Western Kentucky. Here, Howard Porter (with ball) drives for the backboard against Western Kentucky's All-American Jim McDaniels (44). Although Villanova lost to UCLA in the final, the Wildcats' Porter was named tourney MVP.

Right: The trophies pile up for UCLA as Sidney Wicks poses with Wooden and the net. Wooden would soon announce the acquisition of Bill Walton.

5:14
UCL
NATIONAL COLLEGIATE BASKETBALL CHAMPIONSHIP
CHAMPION
TIME

1972

Hard as it was for the Bruins' opponents to believe, the fact remained that the Wizard of Westwood had done it again. San Diegan Bill Walton, at six feet, eleven inches, had led his Helix High School team to 49 straight wins with brilliant passing and rebounding. And he was a player after Wooden's heart – a team player.

As he had done with Alcindor, Wooden surrounded his new star with great back-up players. Keith Wilkes and Larry Farmer were two able forwards. The fine guards consisted of newcomer Greg Lee and veteran Henry Bibby – and the bench was talented as well, with players like Larry Hollyfield and Tommy Curtis. The Bruins even had a future NBA first-round pick sitting on their bench – six-foot, eleven-inch Sven Nater.

Below: *The 1972 NCAA semifinal featured North Carolina and Florida State.*

Right: *UCLA's Bill Walton and FSU's Lawrence McCray (44) tie it on in the title game.*

Far right, below: *The Seminoles fought hard in the classic contest, but lost to the Walton Gang.*

Soon known as the Walton Gang, these 1972 Bruins went about compiling a streak that, before they were done, would have even spoiled UCLA fans shaking their heads – 88 straight games. This was the Team That Could Not Lose.

By tournament time the Bruins and Walton were – needless to say – heavy favorites to win their sixth straight. They were ranked first in the nation, had won 26 straight and were beating opponents by an average of 30 points per game!

Whipping through a Final Four field that included Florida State, North Carolina and Louisville, the Bruins coasted in the title game against the surprising Seminoles. At halftime they led, 50-39. The rest was a foregone conclusion as Walton and Company won NCAA championship number six, 81-76. The redhead from San Diego won the MVP prize in front of a Los Angeles crowd that was ready to elect him Mayor of Basketball.

Larry Farmer later commented on the motivational tactics Wooden used to keep his unconventional star in check: "Coach knew that Bill was a very impressionable guy. If some guy talked to Bill one day and told him the sky was pink, Bill would believe that; and then if he talked to someone the next day who told him the sky was red, Bill would believe that too. Coach wanted us to be individuals and experience college as students, not just as basketball players. In his system, he had rules off and on the court, but within that system he let us be ourselves. I don't think Coach minded Bill expressing his views on war at all. I think he was mad at Bill when Bill got arrested for voicing his views, and I'm sure he told Bill that.

But there was little doubt that, on the court, Walton and Wooden were of one accord.

1973

In 1973 the NCAA again tinkered with its timing format for the semifinals and final – from Thursday-through-Saturday to Saturday-through-Monday. The NCAA tournament had almost completely eclipsed the NIT – it had become the Spring Classic. Played toward the end of March, the final game had become the climax of a two-week basketball festival that began around St. Patrick's Day.

Television was helping to fuel this spring fling. In 1973 TV rights totaled $1,165,755, exceeding the magic million-dollar mark for the first time. NBC reported that the championship game that season was the highest-ranked basketball telecast of all time. It was a prime time affair now, reaching a total audience of 39 million people.

Also in 1973, the NCAA began the practice of granting first-round byes, determining them on the basis of an evaluation of the conference's won-lost record over the past ten years in NCAA play. The first public draw to fill oversubscribed orders for Final Four tickets was administered for the next year's 1974 championship. NCAA tourney basketball was the hottest ticket in town.

Meanwhile, UCLA's consecutive win streak was piling up, game after game. By tournament time it was up to 71 games, and the Bruins had smashed the old record of 60 straight set by Bill Russell's San Francisco team. Every new win was lifting them to a new level. Would they ever lose? It seemed unlikely for the Walton Gang.

Soon they were in the Final Four again. It was a good field. A strong Indiana team, coached by the energetic and frenetic Bobby Knight, was UCLA's semifinal opponent, yet the Bruins prevailed, 70-59, to move into the finals.

Waiting for them was Memphis State, a solid club which had beaten Providence and featured six-foot, nine-inch forward Larry Kenon and a high-scoring guard named Larry Finch. But Bill Walton chose that night to put on a scoring clinic that is still being talked about today. It was one of those nights when Walton simply could not miss. When the title game was over – mercifully for Memphis State – the redhead had hit 21 of 22 from the floor, for a total of 44 points. UCLA had its seventh straight, 87-66, in Walton's MVP performance.

However, there were those who said that unbeaten North Carolina State, under Coach Norm Sloan, was a better team. They had been kept out of postseason play by recruiting violations. The next year would be an interesting one. Could Wooden and Walton pull it off yet again?

Left: John Wooden gets his point across during a time-out in the 1973 NCAA final, as the winning streak rolls on.

Above: Memphis State's Bill Cook (43) drives in a layup, pursued by Providence College's Ernie DiGregorio (15), in the 1973 NCAA semifinal.

Right: Indiana's Quinn Buckner, chain flying, keeps an eye on UCLA's Tommy Curtis in 1973 semifinal action. Indiana was now coached by the irrepressible Bobby Knight.

1974

In 1974 the NCAA changed the tournament's rotation bracket for the first time since its inception in 1939. From now on, East would play West, and the Mideast would take on the Midwest in the national semifinals. Also, the Eastern Collegiate Athletic Conference was divided in order to receive multiple automatic qualification berths in the tournament.

As these changes were made, the rest of the basketball world debated UCLA's chances of an eighth straight NCAA title. It was Bill Walton's senior year – yet the Bruins would meet the North Carolina State Wolfpack in the regular season and perhaps yet again in the tourney. Would they find a way to beat Norm Sloan's squad too?

As the season began, the Bruins easily knocked off Arkansas in a 101-79 opener, and the armchair experts groaned, "Here we go again." But the very next game on their schedule provided a major scare in the form of Maryland. Leading the Terrapins at home in UCLA's Pauley Pavilion, the Bruins had remained in front for most of the game, and clung to a 65-57 lead with just a few minutes left.

Suddenly, however, Maryland began steadily closing the gap – and it took a blocked shot by junior forward Dave Meyers to save the game for the Bruins in the closing seconds, 65-64. The greatest team in college basketball was proving it could be beaten.

North Carolina State's Wolfpack was two games further along in the Bruins' regular season calendar, and all eyes were on the neutral court in St. Louis where the fateful game took place. With an early lead, and Walton in foul trouble, the Bruins let the Wolfpack into the game and struggled to a 54-54 tie in the second half. Then UCLA turned on the afterburners for Walton's return and the game wound up in an 84-66 rout. UCLA had trounced their challenger. At least, so it seemed for the time being.

Later in the season, with the winning streak at an almost unbelievable 88 games, the Bruins and their caravan of followers stopped off in South Bend to take on the Notre Dame Fighting Irish under their colorful coach Digger Phelps. The Irish had proven to be a minor nuisance to the Bruins in the past – but nothing like what happened was anticipated.

With just three minutes left in the game, and holding a 70-59 lead, the Bruins proceeded to go into hibernation. Nothing was hitting for anybody on UCLA. Notre Dame, perceiving that the Bruins were vulnerable, pressed in the final moments to win, 71-70. The news hit the hoops world like an earthquake. Mighty UCLA had fallen! The winning streak was history.

Some thought that, with the enormous burden of the unbeaten streak off its shoulders, the UCLA team might be able to relax and regain its composure. But it was not to be. Back-to-back losses to Oregon State and Oregon confirmed what their fans had feared: the magic was slipping away.

Limping into the tournament which they had dominated for years, the Bruins needed three overtimes to beat Dayton in the first round. By the time they made it to the Final Four, and their semifinal rival North Carolina State, they were looking decidedly like an ordinary team. But that semifinal contest was anything but ordinary.

Norm Sloan's Wolfpack, led by stunning six-foot, four-inch David Thompson, was now the number one ranked team in the nation. Both coaches elected to go with their seven best players only, and the fans were treated to a real thriller in the Greensboro, North Carolina Coliseum as the half wound down to a 35-35 tie.

The second half was more of the same, with both Walton and Thompson producing shot after shot in a trade of brilliant offense. At the buzzer it was still a standoff – 65-65. But, in the second overtime, things began to heat up. UCLA jumped to a seven point lead, the kind of lead the Team That Could Not Lose had usually considered a lock. But they let it slip away as the amazing Wolfpack, with a solid team effort, won the game and the semifinal championship, 80-77. UCLA would not defend its crown.

The Wolfpack would go on to defeat Marquette of Wisconsin, 76-64, in the decidedly anticlimactic final, for its first-ever NCAA crown. UCLA came back to whip Kansas, 78-61, in the consolation game, but for Walton and the Gang, it was over. "We played poorly the last two months of the season," he later remembered. "After the win streak we lost four games we should have won. . . . N.C. State had a great talent and a gamebreaker in David Thompson, but we had a seven-point lead in overtime and made turnovers. We were not as good a team in a slowdown game. Their four-corners slowdown really took us out of it, and I missed a lot of shots around the basket down the stretch."

Thompson was named MVP of the tournament, and the jubilant Wolfpack celebrated with their hometown fans. For UCLA and Coach John Wooden, it was a dismal end to the great college career of a great player, Bill Walton. He had twice been named college basketball player of the year, and now it was on to the pros for the redhead.

But for the Bruins, the end had not quite arrived.

Left: *Finally, some new blood: Marquette's Earl Tatum (43) goes up for a shot as Kansas' Rick Suttle (33) moves in at the semifinal. Meanwhile, North Carolina State was defeating UCLA.*

Above: *It took double overtime, but the Wolfpack bested the Bruins in the 1974 NCAA semifinal. Here, All-American David Thompson (44) pulls down a rebound from UCLA's Dave Meyers (34).*

Right: *He had presided over the win streak, but Bill Walton (left) could not prevent his UCLA team from losing to David Thompson's number one-rated N.C. State Wolfpack.*

1975

Starting in 1975 the NCAA yielded to the inevitable and expanded the tournament field to 32 teams, also adding the policy that teams other than the conference champion could be chosen at large from the same conference. In addition, in a concession to the horde of media people beginning to follow every twist in the tournament from start to finish, dressing rooms were opened to the media after a ten-minute cooling-off period for the players and coaches.

With only one returning starter in forward David Meyers, Wooden was not given much of a chance to come back from the dynasty-toppling defeat of the previous season. Young forward Marques Johnson, six-foot, nine-inch Richard Washington, and starting guards Andre McCarter and Peter Trgovich filled the many holes in the Bruins' arsenal, but the smart money was on Bobby Knight's Indiana Hoosiers to win that year's NCAA tourney.

But the Wizard of Westwood wasn't finished yet. He and his team calmly went about winning their first 12 games, faltering late. However, Indiana had fared even worse, losing its star forward Scott May to a broken arm. UCLA's chances began to look a little better as the tournament began.

Wooden's unknowns beat a strong Arizona team, 89-75, to win their region and climb to the Final Four yet again. Also surviving the expanded field were Kentucky, Louisville and Syracuse. Kentucky took care of the Syracuse Orangemen in one semifinal – but it was up to the Bruins to knock off Louisville, now coached by former Wooden assistant Denny Crum.

In a classic contest, the old master and his younger former assistant traded strategies until the final 48 seconds. With a four-point lead the Cardinals looked ready to win in UCLA's back yard – San Diego. However, the Bruins drew a final burst of strength from somewhere and tied the game on a Marques Johnson hoop just as time ran out. It was on to overtime.

Again neither team seemed to want to take charge – until a great Johnson pass to Washington for a jumper with only ticks left. UCLA had beaten Crum and Louisville, 75-74, to reach the finals.

This team didn't seem strong enough to actually steal the NCAA crown, the experts said. After all, Kentucky Coach Joe B. Hall had an All-American player in six-foot, five-inch Kevin Grevey, and two tall freshmen named Rick Robey and Mike Phillips. Forward Jack "Goose" Givens was also a scoring threat.

Yet, the game remained close until, with seven minutes left, a technical was called on Dave Meyers when he protested his charging call. Wooden, for perhaps the first time in his coaching career, lost his cool, rushing at the officials and having to be restrained by his stunned aides. His emotion seemed to spark the Bruins, as he no doubt intended, and the momentum shifted as they blasted to a 92-85 victory. They had done it again!

It was the tenth title in 12 years for the man who many say is still the best college hoops coach of all time. As the Bruins celebrated Richard Washington's MVP Award, Wooden must have looked back in mild astonishment at what he had accomplished. He had taken the NCAA tourney and made it his – with star players and without them. His record will likely never be broken.

Far left, below: UCLA wasn't finished yet: Marques Johnson's Bruin team captured a tenth title for Wooden.

Below left: Chris Sease (55) of Syracuse blocks a pass by Kentucky's Bob Guyette during 1975 NCAA semifinal play. Kentucky defeated the Orangemen, then lost in the title game to the Bruins.

Above: The Wizard of Westwood: ten NCAA titles in 12 seasons. His record will stand for the ages.

Right: Bruin Richard Washington soars in the final game against Joe B. Hall's Kentucky Wildcats. Washington was named tourney MVP.

1976

The Wooden/Bruin dynasty had ended at an opportune time for the NCAA tournament. With a larger field and no dominant team, competition, parity and fan interest were certain to grow.

Bobby Knight's Indiana team, with Scott May recovered from his season-ending broken arm of the year before, was an early-season favorite. In fact, the Hoosiers played an unbeaten regular season, including several within the tough Big Ten, and rolled into the tournament as official favorites.

A win over Marquette capped their entry into the Final Four – but now the young Hoosiers would be facing tough opponents in UCLA under new Coach Gene Bartow, Rutgers, and Big Ten rival Michigan.

In this bicentennial year, the finals took place in historic Philadelphia and the modern Spectrum. Huge crowds of over 200,000 for the entire tournament made college basketball a part of their bicentennial celebration.

Commentator Billy Packer, a Wake Forest alum, later recalled: "Before the finals, Knight would call me from the broadcast booth over to his team huddle and ask, 'Packer, where the hell is the ACC now?' I thought he had wanted to discuss some important strategy, but before a big game all he was interested in was a little regional one-upmanship."

The first team to enter the title game was speedy Michigan, which ended the Cinderella hopes of sentimental favorite Rutgers, 86-70. Then it was Indiana's turn. They took control of the game early, never letting the Bruins into the flow, and came away with a 65-51 win and the thrill of meeting Big Ten rival Michigan for the NCAA crown. For the first time in NCAA history two teams from the same conference would vie for the title.

In the end, however, the Hoosiers were just too good for Michigan. May had 26 points and tourney MVP Kent Benson had 25 as the Hoosiers built up a 35-29 half-time lead and the eventual 86-68 victory. For Bobby Knight, the former Ohio State Buckeye who had played in the Final Four himself, it was a thrill he would never forget – and he vowed to be back. And he was.

Below left: *Michigan Wolverine Phil Hubbard is double-teamed by the Rutgers defense. Michigan ended the hopes of Cinderella Rutgers in the 1976 NCAA tourney semifinals, 86-70.*

Below: *Michigan's Phil Hubbard (35) and Rutgers' Abdel Anderson (54) jump for the ball during tense semifinal competition, as the bicentennial crowd looks on at the Philadelphia Spectrum.*

Right: *Tournament MVP Kent Benson paced the Hoosiers to an NCAA title for Coach Bobby Knight. Benson scored 25 points in the 86-68 win over Michigan.*

1977

In the 1977 NCAA tournament's Final Four the entire nation watched as little Marquette University in Wisconsin, and its emotional coach, Al McGuire, had its day in the sun. Courtesy of NBC's 23 hours and 18 minutes of tournament programming, the fans felt a part of the action as never before.

As Billy Packer, a friend of McGuire's, recalled, "McGuire inherited a 20-game loser and turned it into a 20-game winner. He had a knack for attracting city-tough players to Wisconsin, although he was never a great recruiter. He took all that inner-city energy and harnessed it into the picture of precision basketball, teethed with a spirit-breaking defense.

"By 1977, he had won the NIT and been to eight NCAA tournaments, rising to the finals in 1974 before losing to N.C. State. But, as he often reminds me, Al felt basketball; he didn't live it and breathe it. He was never a hoops junkie. So early in the '77 season, while his team was struggling and appeared headed nowhere, he grew weary of the grind and announced his retirement, effective at the close of the campaign . . . what happened from there was pure storybook."

The Final Four field that year also included a strong North Carolina team, plus the University of Nevada-Las Vegas (UNLV) and the University of North Carolina at Charlotte.

The title game, with North Carolina heavily favored, featured a powerful trio of Tar Heels in Walter Davis, Mike O'Koren and Phil Ford. Yet scrappy Marquette, led by star guard Butch Lee, prevailed, pulling off an unlikely 67-59 upset. In the closing minutes of the final game of his coaching career, as Coach McGuire realized the crown was theirs, he wept openly. Twice his Warriors had been regional runners-up (one game from the Final Four), and in 1974 they had made it to the finals – only to be beaten by N.C. State.

But now the title was theirs, and as the jubilant fans celebrated with McGuire and his players, it seemed that now anyone could dream of winning the crown. If Marquette could do it, coaches and fans realized, it was now a wide-open race.

Above left: *Marquette fans make their statement during the 1977 NCAA final. Marquette's emotional coach, Al McGuire, won an NCAA title in 1977, then became a well-known color commentator for college basketball.*

Above: *Television was bringing NCAA action into a record number of homes. Fan interest was at an all-time high.*

Left: *Bernard Toone does the honors as Marquette celebrates with the traditional cutting down of the net.*

Right: *North Carolina's Phil Ford jumps for the ball in NCAA semifinal action against UNLV.*

1978

In 1978 the NCAA instituted, for the first time, a "seeding" process for individual teams. A maximum of four automatic qualifying conference teams were seeded in each of the four regional brackets. These teams were seeded in the tournament based on the won-lost percentages of their respective conferences in the NCAA tourney during the previous five years.

At-large seeding in each region was based on a team's current won-lost record, the strength of its schedule, and the eligibility status of its athletes in the post-season. With each new refinement, the NCAA was attempting to make it a fairer contest. Small regional powerhouses, as well as independents like Notre Dame, DePaul and Miami of Ohio, could thus have the same chance of favorable seeding in the tournament as did the major conference champs.

With NCAA Productions televising all the regional semifinal games and all other tourney contests, it was no wonder that this year's Final Four competition, to be held in St. Louis' Checkerdome, was so eagerly awaited!

The 1978 Final Four featured an extremely strong and well-balanced field of Digger Phelps' Notre Dame, Arkansas, Duke and Kentucky. Jack "Goose" Givens was now a legitimate star for Joe B. Hall's Kentucky Wildcats, but Duke boasted Gene Banks, Mike Gminski and Jim Spanarkel.

But it was Kentucky which prevailed, riding a red-hot shooting display by Givens, who seemed to sink every shot – scoring 18 of his 27 field goal tries. His 41-point performance set the Checkerdome on fire and gave Kentucky a minor upset victory over Duke, 94-88.

Far left: *Scrappy Arkansas battles Joe B. Hall's Kentucky Wildcats, the eventual champions, in NCAA semifinal action.*

Below left: *Duke's Mike Gminski sparked a powerful Duke offense. His team fell to Kentucky and red-hot Jack Givens in the '78 NCAA final.*

Above: *Coach Joe B. Hall of Kentucky carried on the proud tradition of his predecessor, Adolph Rupp.*

Above: *The Kentucky Wildcats' All-American Rick Robeyn comes down with the rebound against Duke in the title game. Kentucky's basketball tradition originates in the mountain spirit of its people, according to Joe B. Hall.*

Later, Kentucky Coach Joe B. Hall talked about the enduring basketball tradition at his school: "I guess there was a commitment to basketball early in its involvement that led Kentucky to develop this rich tradition. The administrators at the University, back before Coach Rupp, recognized basketball as a kind of salvation for Kentucky. The small rural communities on the high school level did not play football in the state of Kentucky. Many of the schools were so inaccessible back up in the hollows that they just couldn't get that many kids together to have a football team. Basketball became a way of life in the Kentucky mountains and in Eastern Kentucky. That influence and public acceptance of basketball encouraged the administration at the University to support basketball in the very early stages of the game."

Givens' outstanding MVP performance in the '78 final looked to be a standard that would be hard to equal for those who came after him. But that was before Larry Bird and Earvin "Magic" Johnson came along.

1979

The NCAA tournament bracket was expanded again, to 40 teams in 1979 – with all teams being seeded. The Division 1 Men's Basketball Committee elected to assign three-man officiating crews for all future tournament games. Other news concerned tickets to the yearly spectacle. Complimentary tickets to the championship game had been eliminated the year before, and now a public lottery-type drawing for Final Four game tickets was held for the first time.

Meanwhile, two distinctly different players, relative unknowns before the season began, would burst into the NCAA spotlight with their respective schools. They were six-foot, nine-inch forward Larry Bird from Indiana State University, and six-foot, nine-inch Earvin Johnson, whom everyone called "Magic" – for reasons which would become obvious.

Larry Bird, having grown up poor in Indiana, had first elected to join Bobby Knight at Indiana. Yet, inexplicably, he had dropped out, then later entered the far smaller school, Indiana State, which did not really even have a major basketball program. At least, not until Larry.

Earvin Johnson, raised in East Lansing, Michigan as one of ten children, had been one of those pesky youngsters – always the youngest on the court, trying to pick up tips from the older players. He was an outstanding dribbler and ball-handler at a very young age as a result. Following his hometown friend, Jay Vincent, to Michigan State, Magic Johnson was immediately a starter, since freshmen were now allowed on the varsity.

Almost inevitably, the two stars – Bird and Johnson – found themselves on a collision course in the Final Four. Bird had already been drafted by the Boston Celtics, but had told the club he wanted to return to Indiana State. Cigar-chomping Red Auerbach of the Celtics was willing to wait.

During the 1978-79 season Bird was averaging 29 points and 15 rebounds per game, and showing terrific passing ability from his forward slot. The unheralded Sycamores were setting the college basketball world ablaze with their unbeaten season – becoming the surprise number one-ranked team in the nation as tournament time approached.

Meanwhile, for Magic Johnson and the rest of Coach Jud Heathcote's Michigan State Spartans, the season was rocky. Center Jay Vincent had been injured early in the season, and the Spartans had to win 15 of their last 16 games to crack the top ten rankings. An NCAA field expanded to 40 teams made MSU a long shot at best.

As the tournament began, Larry Bird was nursing a thumb he'd broken in the last game of the Missouri Valley tournament. However, even with a sore digit Bird and his able Sycamore teammates lit up the Midwest regional, finally besting a tough Arkansas team, with its All-American Sidney Moncrief. Bird had run wild, scoring 25 points in the first 27 minutes and trying to hold off the surging Moncrief and the Razorbacks. Indiana State won the close-fought game, 73-71, and were, surprisingly, in the Final Four.

Michigan State had an easier victory, 80-68, over the Fighting Irish of Notre Dame, to reach the Final Four on Spartan forward Greg Kelser's 34 points.

The Spartans' semifinal opponents were the Pennsylvania Quakers, who quickly realized that they were in way over their heads. They folded early and MSU was in the title game with a 101-67 cruise.

However, Indiana State's semifinal game was against DePaul, featuring coach and elder statesman Ray Meyer – the same DePaul coach who had nurtured George Mikan in the 1940s. DePaul, with budding freshman star Mark Aguirre, made it close all the way, but when Aguirre missed a late shot Indiana State got the ball and Larry Bird had done it again, posting 35 points and 16 rebounds.

And so it was that the two stars – Bird and Johnson – would meet in the final game. Both appeared headed for the pros the following year, so the title game was hyped as the battle of the future NBA stars. Salt Lake City's Special Events Center was the venue, and more than 15,000 fanatics saw the clash.

Coach Heathcote had instituted a trapping zone defense to contain Bird, at the same time springing Johnson and Kelsern to score big. Indiana State drew 22 trips to the foul line from MSU's rompin' stompin' defense, but converted only ten of them.

In the end, Bird was a one-man team, while Magic Johnson had more help from a talented MSU cast. The final score was 75-64 in favor of Michigan State. Magic Johnson earned MVP honors on 24 points, while Bird had a somewhat mediocre (for him) performance with only 19. Bird and Johnson would later renew their rivalry many times in the 1980s as stars of the Boston Celtics and Los Angeles Lakers, respectively.

Meanwhile, the college basketball world would soon be rocking to the 1980s beat of the Parade of Stars.

Left: *Tournament MVP Earvin "Magic" Johnson of Michigan State scores against Indiana State, en route to leading his Spartan teammates to the 1979 NCAA title.*

Above: *Indiana State's Larry Bird gets off a shot in the title game. Bird showed his explosive talent in NCAA showcase games.*

Right: *Larry Bird dribbles down the court. More than 15,000 fans saw the matchup of Larry Bird against Magic Johnson, which many say ushered in the modern era of college basketball.*

1980

In 1980 the NCAA tourney expanded again, this time to 48 teams – 24 automatic qualifiers and 24 at-large teams. The top 16 seeds received byes to the second round of what was now becoming a mammoth tournament. The final game would soon be pushing into the first week in April, but the fans didn't seem to mind.

Also, the limit of two teams from the same conference allowed in the tourney was lifted, so that the selection committee would have the most flexibility possible to balance each regional bracket, as well as select the best at-large entrants.

In 1980 Denny Crum, early disciple of John Wooden, finally attained the NCAA crown he had worked for. His Louisville Cardinal team beat an upstart UCLA Bruins squad, after UCLA had done them the courtesy of knocking off number one-ranked DePaul in the second round.

DePaul and star Mark Aguirre had matured and were the practical, as well as sentimental, favorite to take it all. Ray Meyer, the dean of college coaches, was retiring, and fans everywhere wanted to see him win the tournament just once before he handed over the coaching reins to his son, Joey Meyer. But it was not to be. The Bruins capped a lackluster regular season by peaking in the playoffs, and knocked off the Blue Demons, 77-71. Among the future NBA stars on that 1980 Bruins team: Kiki Vanderweghe and Rod Foster.

From there, the Bruins continued to blast through the field, beating Ohio State and finally Clemson to reach the Final Four. Louisville, Iowa and Purdue stood in the way of yet another NCAA championship for UCLA.

The Bruins did succeed in squeaking by Purdue, 67-62, to reach the title game. Meanwhile, Louisville knocked off Coach Lute Olsen's strong Iowa team and its high-flying Ronnie Lester – to complete a double-dashing of Big Ten hopes for an NCAA title.

Then Crum's squad, paced by Darrell Griffith and freshman forward Rodney McCray, outshot the Bruins 59-54 to attain the NCAA championship. Griffith was named MVP. A footnote: the Bruins' participation in the tournament was later vacated by the NCAA.

Left: *Louisville, paced by tournament MVP Darrell Griffith (left), outshoots the Iowa Hawkeyes in the NCAA semifinal, en route to their 1980 championship.*

Right: *Darrell Griffith in finals action. Denny Crum's Louisville Cardinal team beat a tough UCLA Bruin squad to take the 1980 NCAA crown.*

Below: *Louisville Coach Denny Crum watches from the bench as his underdog Cardinals make their way through the tourney. Early disciple of John Wooden, Crum would taste victory in 1980.*

35
11
14

1981

The level of college basketball talent in the U.S. may have reached its high-water mark in 1981. A partial list of stars who were thrilling fans: Isiah Thomas at Indiana, James Worthy and Sam Perkins at North Carolina, seven-foot, four-inch Ralph Sampson at Virginia, Mark Aguirre and Terry Cummings at DePaul, Danny Ainge at Brigham Young, Kelly Tripucka at Notre Dame and Sam Bowie at Kentucky.

However, individual stars don't make it to the Final Four: teams do. When the early-round hooplas began dying down, four teams advanced to the Final Four. They were Louisiana State, Virginia, North Carolina and Bobby Knight's Indiana Hoosiers.

It was an unusual year for the tournament. For instance, the finals were disrupted by the news that President Reagan had been shot and wounded, and tournament officials huddled with the network and the two schools involved, to decide whether the game should be postponed. NCAA officials decide to go ahead with the game upon learning that the President was out of immediate danger.

Bobby Knight's Hoosiers would play North Carolina

Left: North Carolina's Sam Perkins (41) fights for the ball in the 1981 title game against Indiana. The level of college talent was at an all-time high in 1981.

Above: Indiana Coach Bobby Knight was only too happy to point out any lapses in officiating.

Right: Isiah Thomas was Knight's ace in the hole, as the Hoosiers claimed their 1981 NCAA crown with shooting like this. Thomas, with his 23 points and 11 rebounds in the title game, won MVP honors.

Far right: Howard Carter gets off a shot in tournament competition. Louisiana State battled gamely, but was eliminated in the semifinal by the eventual champion, Indiana.

for the championship. If Indiana won, they would be the first national champ to finish the regular season with as many as nine losses. But that statistic did nothing to dampen Knight's enthusiasm or desire to win. In addition to an electrifying guard in Isiah Thomas, the hyperactive coach had other solid players, including Ray Tolbert.

Knight's Hoosiers had had little trouble against Louisiana State, handling them, 67-49. Meanwhile, North Carolina was polishing off the University of Virginia and player-of-the-year Ralph Sampson, 78-65. North Carolina's patient, crafty Dean Smith would prove an entertaining complement to Knight.

The Tar Heels held the slimmest of leads over Indiana early in the title game, but the Hoosiers had gained a one-point edge at the half. From there, the lead grew steadily more comfortable for Indiana fans.

Isiah Thomas' 23 points, plus 11 rebounds from Ray Tolbert, paced the Hoosiers to a 63-50 victory and Knight's second NCAA crown. Thomas won MVP honors, while Dean Smith and the Tar Heels went home to lick their wounds. The following season, with a new freshman named Michael Jordan, they would be back.

1982

In 1982 CBS was awarded the television rights to the NCAA championship, and the "selection show," featuring the selection of the 48-team tournament, was shown on national TV for the first time. That tradition has evolved, until today extravagant "selection parties" are arranged by fans of schools who hope to be at-large selections by the NCAA committee.

North Carolina had indeed come back. They had not only retained Worthy and Perkins but had welcomed freshman guard Michael Jordan – and they held the number one AP ranking for most of the 1981-82 season.

They would have a worthy opponent in Washington D.C.'s Georgetown University, coached by John Thompson and featuring newly-recruited seven-footer Patrick Ewing. These two schools, representing the Atlantic Coast and Big East Conference, would be joined by Houston and Denny Crum's Louisville in the 1982 Final Four. Houston also boasted an interesting new recruit: a young seven-foot Nigerian named Akeem Olajuwon.

Excitement built as the four teams prepared to play in New Orleans' huge Superdome, with a capacity of 60,000 fans. In reality, the final game would draw more than 61,000 fans – to dwarf any crowd ever assembled for a Final Four event. To many observers, the site selection of the Superdome marked the recognition that the NCAA tourney had attained the status of the World Series and Super Bowl as a major athletic event in the U.S.

The semifinal contests proved exciting. On the strength of Sam Perkins' 25 points and 10 rebounds, North Carolina and its star-studded front line whipped Houston, 68-63. In the other matchup, Georgetown and stellar guard Eric "Sleepy" Floyd beat Louisville in a bitter clash, 50-46. The winners prepared to do battle in the final game.

Left: North Carolina Coach Dean Smith's star-studded team held off the charging Georgetown Hoyas to claim the 1982 crown.

Above: Michael Jordan stopped by North Carolina en route to immortality in the NBA. In the '82 title game, freshman Jordan showed he was a clutch player, his 15-foot basket in the final seconds making the difference.

Above right: Michael Jordan lays one up for the Tar Heels during the NCAA final. North Carolina's battle with Georgetown for the title reached the last few seconds, when the Tar Heels prevailed, 63-62.

Right: Houston's Larry Micheaux gets off a shot in the NCAA semifinals, where Houston lost to eventual champion North Carolina.

Far right: Clash of the Titans: Hoya Patrick Ewing battles for the ball with Tar Heel Sam Perkins.

The game's first five minutes had the fans on their feet. Each of North Carolina's first four drives with the ball ended with Patrick Ewing slapping the ball away and being charged with goaltending. Youthful exuberance and natural talent on Ewing's part made the score 8-0 before the Tar Heels had made a shot from the floor.

Then John Thompson's Hoyas settled down and took the lead. Tar Heel Worthy had a hot hand and tallied 18 points by halftime, but the Hoyas still entered the locker room with a 32-31 lead. In the second half the lead bounced back and forth, and it became obvious that this one would be close. Worthy, Ewing, Floyd and Jordan all sank crucial shots in the final six minutes. With 15 seconds to go the score was 63-62, Tar Heels.

Time for one more rush, thought the Hoyas. But guard Fred Brown lost the ball to James Worthy on an ill-advised pass. Worthy missed a couple of last-second free throws that would have iced the game, but the Tar Heels hung on to win 63-62. They were national champs, and Worthy was awarded MVP honors.

The walls were vibrating as the fans went wild – yet television cameras caught John Thompson administering a comforting hug to a dejected Brown, who felt he had let his team down. It simply added to the drama of this event, one of the most amazing tournament finishes anyone could remember.

1983

In 1983 the NCAA added an opening round that required the representatives of eight automatic qualifying conferences to compete for four positions in the 52-team tournament bracket. This permitted the committee to retain a 48-team bracket – evenly balanced with 24 automatic qualifiers and 24 at-large choices – yet grant automatic qualifications to each of the 28 teams that received it the year before. The 16 top-seeded teams received byes to the second round.

The format was established which exists today: the tournament began the third weekend in March, regional championships took place on the fourth Saturday and Sunday, and the Final Four events (the national semifinals and final) the following Saturday and Monday.

Prime time media coverage reflected the importance of this event. Record viewership for the Final Four in virtually each successive year guaranteed even greater media interest. Partially in response to the needs of television, the tournament committee determined that any facility hosting the final must have a minimum of 17,000 seats.

Left: *Akeem Olajuwon (34) guards the net. Houston's Phi Slamma Jamma met its match in the 1983 title game against the North Carolina State Wolfpack.*

Above: *North Carolina's effervescent Coach Jim Valvano celebrates after the Wolfpack's upset victory over the Houston Cougars for the NCAA title.*

Above right: *A team portrait of the 1983 NCAA Champions: North Carolina State. The Wolfpack included future NBA star Lorenzo Charles (middle row, fourth from right).*

The heavy favorites in the 1983 tournament were the Houston Cougars. With the Nigerian, Akeem Olajuwon, a force in the middle, Coach Guy Lewis had assembled a group of players who were busily redefining the art of the slam-dunk. They called themselves "Phi Slamma Jamma" – and the nickname stuck. Meanwhile, they were compiling a 27-2 regular season record.

Yet the NCAA title was to belong to the North Carolina State Wolfpack, coached by the effervescent Jim Valvano. They weren't a great team, but they had taken the ACC tourney, upsetting both North Carolina and Virginia. In the process, they had apparently made believers out of themselves as well, because they were now playing great basketball.

After continuing their Cinderella run at the crown by knocking off Georgia, 67-60, they prepared to meet the official favorites – the Houston Cougars featuring Phi Slamma Jamma! On Olajuwon's 21-point, 22-rebound explosion in the semifinal against Louisville, the Cougars had won handily, 94-81, and now wanted what they thought was theirs by right.

They were as surprised as the 17,000 gathered at the University of New Mexico's Pit when N.C. State managed to enter the locker room at halftime with a 33-25 lead. But Houston reeled off a 15-2 spurt early in the second half, seeming to turn the tide.

Then, with nine minutes left in the game, Cougar Coach Lewis tried to slow things down a bit. The Wolfpack, sensing the strategy, found a second wind and tied the score at 52 with barely two minutes left – and still the Cougars were in a stall.

With seconds left on the clock, Cougar Dereck Whittenberg tried an off-balance shot. It was grabbed out of thin air by Wolfpack sophomore Lorenzo Charles, who stuffed it home at the buzzer. The upset darlings of the 1983 NCAA tourney, N.C. State, had won, 54-52, in a dramatic contest. They were dancing in the streets of Raleigh, North Carolina.

Houston's Akeem Olajuwon was accorded the MVP title, but must have found it a hollow achievement. Houston settled for runner-up, followed by Louisville and Georgia.

1984

In 1984 the NCAA bracket stood at 54 teams, with one additional open-round game established. It required ten automatic qualifiers to compete for five positions.

For the first time, awards were presented to all participating teams in the championship. The site that season would be Seattle's Kingdome.

It was the year of the really big man. Olajuwon at Houston and Patrick Ewing at Georgetown were still in school, and Kentucky's twin towers, seven-foot, one-inch Sam Bowie and six-foot, eleven-inch Mel Turpin, were dominating. These three super teams, plus surprising Virginia, comprised the Final Four that year – one of the most glittering in recent memory.

Houston had some trouble defeating Virginia's stalling strategy, but looked toward the title game with a 49-47 win in OT. The other semifinal pitted Kentucky and Georgetown – and it was a barnburner.

Kentucky came out like they had been shot from a cannon – posting a 27-15 lead after 11 minutes. Ewing was on the Hoya bench with three fouls, and John Thompson knew something had to change. He called for the full court press, and by halftime the Hoyas had cut the lead to 29-22.

In the second half the Kentucky Wildcats played more like pussycats, and the Hoyas were on fire. They ran the score to 34-29 before Kentucky ever scored, and coasted to a 53-40 victory. It was one of the biggest halftime turnarounds in the history of the tournament.

The NCAA final against Houston followed a similar pattern. Houston led early, but Georgetown came storming back to take a 40-30 lead into the dressing room at the half.

Foul trouble spelled disaster for Olajuwon and the Cougars in the second half. Drawing his fourth personal foul just 23 seconds into the period, Olajuwon watched helplessly as Georgetown took charge under the basket and took the NCAA crown, 84-75. John Thompson's Hoyas were national champs, and Patrick Ewing took MVP honors as a Kingdome crowd of 38,471 roared its approval.

Left: *Kentucky's Sam Bowie competes for a rebound with Hoya Mike Graham (50) during 1984 semifinal action. Georgetown defeated Kentucky, then went on to win it all.*

Above: *Georgetown Coach John Thompson directs his team from the bench. Thompson has been a strong and visible leader for the Hoyas – as well as an advocate of education reform in college basketball.*

Right: *Houston's Akeem Olajuwon comes up against Georgetown's Patrick Ewing in a classic confrontation during the 1984 title game. The Hoyas took it, 84-75, and Ewing was named MVP.*

EWING
AKEEM
35
WE

1985

In 1985 the tourney bracket reached its present level of 64 teams, and all first-round byes were eliminated. Also, the committee juggled a number of the regions, and the number of automatic qualifiers was capped at 30, for a five-year period which extends through 1990.

It was clear that, for the time being at least, the Big East was one of the dominant conferences in college basketball. Defending NCAA tournament champ Georgetown, Syracuse and St. John's all hailed from the Big East – and so did Villanova. The Villanova Wildcats had been considered poor relations in the conference, and no one expected them to come to the forefront, much less win the title.

The 1985 Final Four proved to be a Big East reunion, as Georgetown, St. John's and the upstart Villanova team made it that far, along with Memphis State. With Georgetown a heavy favorite to repeat, no one was very surprised when they beat pesky conference rival St. John's, 77-59. Reggie Williams scored 20 and Ewing tallied 16. With the Hoyas' only major competitor out of the way, said the experts, it almost didn't matter who won the other semifinal.

Right: *Villanova Coach Rollie Massimino is carried off the court after his team's NCAA title win over Georgetown. Massimino proved his Wildcats were no longer the "poor relations" of the Big East Conference.*

Below: *Tournament MVP Ed Pinckney of Philadelphia's Villanova University leads a raucous celebration after the Wildcats brought home the national championship trophy in 1985.*

Right: *Georgetown fans waited for Patrick Ewing (33) and the Hoyas to pull away – but it never happened. In the upset final, Villanova won by two points.*

But Villanova, coached by Rollie Massimino, pulled off another surprise win over Memphis State, 52-45, and gamely prepared to face the Hoya powerhouse. No one gave them two nickels for their chances.

Yet when the 1985 NCAA title game began, it was Massimino's Wildcats who looked cool as cucumbers, as they hit shots from every spot on the court, facing down the Georgetown press behind point guard Gary McLain.

Also, six-foot, nine-inch Ed Pinckney had been assigned the formidable task of trying to stop Patrick Ewing, and he was succeeding. When the halftime buzzer sounded, Villanova led, 29-28.

In the second half, fans at Kentucky's Rupp Arena were waiting for Georgetown to explode, but it never happened. Villanova's bend-but-don't-break defense stood them well in the closing minutes, and as John Thompson paced and fumed on the sideline, the Villanova Wildcats held on to the slimmest of two-point leads until time ran out on Georgetown. They had won, 66-64.

And it was no fluke. Villanova had hit on 78.6 percent from the field – 90 percent in the second half. Pinckney was named MVP for his 16 points and 6 rebounds. But it was a team effort, as a Massimino pointed out.

With the two big men, Ewing and Olajuwon, gone to the NBA, the college basketball world had to be wondering: who's next?

1986

In 1986 the tournament committee ruled that regional competition would be played at neutral sites. If an institution selected to host was a participant, that school would be bracketed in another region so that they wouldn't be playing at their own school.

Meanwhile, there was little doubt in many fans' minds that the 1986 tournament winner would be Duke. With All-American juard Johnny Dawkins, the Blue Devils were 28-2 for the season, and it was no surprise when they stormed into the Final Four under Coach Mike Krzyzewski.

The other participants were Louisville, LSU and Kansas. Denny Crum's Cardinals looked good as they topped LSU, 88-77, while Duke beat a tough Kansas team, 71-67, behind 24 Dawkins points.

Duke was still favored to win, but fans had taken note of Louisville's senior forward, Billy Thompson, senior guard Milt Wagner, and six-foot, nine-inch freshman center Pervis Ellison. One might have expected the newcomer to wilt under Final Four pressure in his very first season, but Ellison's nickname was "Never Nervous."

The title game stayed close, with Duke leading 37-34 at the half. Hawkins' jump shot four seconds before the halftime buzzer had done the trick, and fans everywhere were learning why he had been named Naismith Player of the Year.

However, during the early part of the second half, no one took charge. Finally, the freshman Ellison made his move for Louisville. With four minutes remaining he scored the go-ahead basket, then blocked another shot with 40 seconds to go to give Louisville a 68-65 lead. They were able to hang on and win, 72-67, for Denny Crum's second NCAA title. After the game the jubilant coach had this to say about Ellison, "It's unbelievable a freshman can handle that kind of pressure and play as well as he did."

In becoming tournament MVP, Pervis Ellison had proved he was indeed "Never Nervous." He finished with 25 points and 11 rebounds, to Dawkins' 24 for Duke.

Left: *After practice before an opening-round NCAA game, Louisville's freshman forward David Robinson flashes the "We are number one" sign. Later, his team would prove him right.*

Above: *Louisville Coach Denny Crum won his second national title on patience and the cool skills of freshman center Pervis Ellison. In the hard-fought NCAA final, Louisville downed Duke, 72-69.*

Right: *Pervis Ellison's nickname was "Never Nervous" – even before a key free throw. With 25 points and 11 rebounds in the title game, Ellison was named tournament MVP.*

Left: Rony Seikaly of Syracuse (left) battles for the loose ball with Rick Calloway (20) and Dean Garrett (22) of the Indiana Hoosiers during first-half action in the NCAA title game.

Below: Tourney MVP Keith Smart (23) of the Hoosiers is about to sink a key shot in the closing moments of Indiana's NCAA championship victory over Syracuse. Orangeman Greg Monroe (with outstretched arm) tries a block.

Right: New Orleans' monstrous Superdome was the site of the 1987 NCAA championship – and the throng of fans loved every minute of it.

Below right: Jubilant Indiana Coach Bobby Knight celebrates being back on top of the college basketball heap.

The 1987 season saw the NCAA institute the three-point field goal, taking a cue from the pro game. It made the tournament games more exciting, and may even have influenced the outcome of the final that year.

Championship team members were awarded ten-carat gold rings beginning that year, with the other three Final Four teams sporting silver rings. Also, drug testing for the players of all 64 tournament teams was begun in 1987.

The three-point shot was used to great effect by two of the Final Four teams that season. The Big East's Providence College, coached by Rick Patino, could hit long jumpers, and they used them to attain the Final Four. The Runnin' Rebels of the University of Nevada-Las Vegas could shoot for three points, and could also dominate from inside. Coached by the towel-chewing bald man, Jerry Tarkanian, UNLV's Runnin' Rebels boasted stellar guard Freddie Banks, and also Armon Gilliam, who played tough underneath.

Coach Bobby Knight and Hoosiers were back, featuring All-American Steve Alford. Syracuse was the fourth finalist, and was presumed to be the weakest from the outside.

Providence College and Syracuse University, the Big East rivals, did battle in one semifinal, with the solid Orangemen posting a 77-63 victory to eliminate the Cinderella Friars from Providence.

A classic shootout between UNLV and Indiana saw Freddie Banks score 38 points and Armon Gilliam score 32 for the Runnin' Rebels in a losing cause, as Alford posted 33 in the Hoosiers' 97-93 victory to advance to the title game.

The finals were back in the Superdome that year, and the fans jammed in to check out the excitement and the effect of the three-point-rule. Once again the NCAA title game was a close, hard-fought, elbow-banging affair. The Orangemen took the lead early behind the fine play of Rony Seikaly, but Indiana ran into the locker room clinging to the slimmest of margins at the half, 34-33. In the final seconds of the game, with Syracuse ahead by a point, the ball went to Hoosier Keith Smart on the baseline, and he sank it to give Indiana, and Knight, a heart-stopping 74-73 NCAA championship. Smart won MVP honors. Meanwhile, Alford had been 8 for 15 from the floor in that final game – but seven of ten from three-point range. The new ruling, and Alford's performance, had made the difference for Indiana.

1988

Left: *Kansas' Danny Manning drives on Oklahoma's Harvey Grant during first-half action in the 1988 title game. Manning's stellar performance led the Jayhawks to an 83-79 victory and earned him the MVP Award.*

Above: *University of Kansas Coach Larry Brown would lead his squad to the national championship in 1988 before defecting to the NBA.*

Right: *Lute Olsen's Arizona squad bowed early to the Oklahoma Sooners in the 1988 semifinal.*

In 1988 yet another underdog team would claim the title on the strength and guts of one player. That player was Danny Manning of the University of Kansas. Coach Larry Brown felt he had the best player in the country in Manning, and many experts agreed.

The six-foot, eleven-inch forward was compared to Magic Johnson – only he was two inches taller. A superb ball-handler and scoring machine, he was so highly touted that many wondered whether he would finish his education at Kansas before turning pro.

Manning had the job of carrying his Jayhawk club for most of the year. In fact, with 11 losses, the team wasn't even sure of an NCAA bid. But it came, and Manning proved he was ready.

In the Midwest regional final, against opponent Kansas State, Manning and his team began to show their promise. Winning 71-58 in what was considered a mild upset, the Jayhawks were now in the Final Four, and headed for Kansas City's Kemper Arena for the rest of the tournament.

The other three Final Four winners that year were Coach Billy Tubbs' fast-breaking Oklahoma Sooners, who were favored to win it all, plus Arizona and Duke.

In the semifinal against Duke, Manning scored 25 points and came through in the clutch to pace the Jayhawks in a 66-59 win. Duke, a seemingly perennial Final Four participant, went home disappointed again. Oklahoma had little difficulty beating Arizona, 86-78, and now they waited for Kansas.

The Kemper Arena was no Superdome, but the 16,000 fans yelled themselves hoarse as they watched Manning and the Jayhawks take on Oklahoma's Harvey Grant and Stacy King. Oklahoma just couldn't get by Manning. Running wild and shooting from all over the court, Manning forced the Sooners to change their offensive strategy, and it hurt them.

Kansas took the lead for keeps in the second half, and with Manning exhausted but sensing victory, they posted an 83-79 win for their NCAA crown.

Manning's performance, which ranks among the most outstanding individual performances in the history of the tournament, netted him 31 points and the MVP Award. Subsequently he was named college player of the year, and was picked number one in the NBA draft. He had proved that taller men could still be quick and flashy.

The tournament was becoming wide open, which heightened fan and media interest. With upset after upset in the semifinals and final, it seemed that whatever team peaked at the right time had a chance to be NCAA champs.

ARIZONA
23
35
ARIZONA
11
14

1989

In 1989 the NCAA made a number of adjustments. A moratorium enacted in '84 to limit participants to 30 automatic qualification conference champions and 34 at-large teams through the 1989 championship was expanded through 1998. This will ensure relative stability and will let all teams wishing to qualify know exactly what they have to do to be selected.

Also, a rotation bracket was established, with East vs. West, Midwest vs. Southeast in 1989; East vs. Southeast, West vs. Midwest in 1990; and East vs. Midwest, Southeast vs. West in 1991. The cycle will continue in 1992 with East vs. West and Midwest vs. Southeast.

It was determined that awards for the national runner-up would be presented in the dressing room immediately following the championship game. In addition, it was ruled that neutral courts would be used in all rounds of the championship.

This was to be the season of the Cinderella Michigan Wolverines – a tournament that was dominated by personality. On the strength of dead-eye shooting by Glen Rice, and an assistant coach with the wisdom to let well enough alone, the Wolverines became national champs. But it wasn't easy.

Michigan coach Bill Frieder ended a long career at Michigan by accepting the position at Arizona State, announcing the move just as the tournament began. He had obviously assumed that Michigan Athletic Director Bo Schembechler would want him to remain in his position through the tournament. He thought wrong. "We want a Michigan man coaching a Michigan team," he told reporters. Hell hath no fury like a Schembechler scorned. So tournament coaching duties fell to Frieder's quiet and unassuming assistant, Steve Fisher.

With no time to get nervous, Fisher's squad, led by

Below left: *A jubilant Michigan Wolverine team, 1989 national champs, records their success for posterity. The Cinderella team defeated Seton Hall by one point in the 1989 NCAA title game.*

Right: *Tournament MVP Glen Rice (right) and rising talent Rumeal Robinson celebrate after their exciting championship game.*

Above: *Michigan's Steve Fisher: "unbeaten, untied, and the happiest man alive!"*

Rice as the Big Ten's all-time leading scorer and featuring rising talents Rumeal Robinson and center Terry Mills, blazed through the tournament. The other Final Four teams were Seton Hall, Illinois and Duke. Then in the final game the amazing Wolverines pulled off a heart-stopping 80-79 victory against P. J. Carlesimo's talented Seton Hall Pirates.

Rice's brilliance in the tournament would earn him the MVP prize, but other crack Wolverine players such as Robinson were playing the game of their young lives. In fact, it was Robinson's collision with Pirate Gerald Greene, and two clutch free throws with three seconds left in the title game which won the day for Michigan.

"I ought to retire now," Fisher said after the game. "Steve Fisher is unbeaten, untied, and the happiest man alive." He was the first interim, first rookie, and first unbeaten coach ever to take the world's most famous basketball tournament. A few days later, he was also Michigan's official head basketball coach.

1990

As the NCAA tournament sails into the 1990s, it will be tough to top the Final Four performance of the 1990 UNLV Runnin' Rebels. Coach Jerry Tarkanian, nicknamed "Tark the Shark" by fans and the media, led his crack squad through the tourney as the number one seed in the Western Region and the odds-on favorite to win it all, after doomed appearances in 1977 and 1987 Final Four play. Duke, Arkansas and Georgia Tech stood in UNLV's way as the other 1990 Final Four teams – but only briefly.

After surviving a halftime deficit of 53-46 against the Georgia Tech Yellow Jackets, Tark's Rebels stormed back to win, 90-81, over the finesse play of Tech in the semifinal. Tech was later unkindly dubbed "the only team to lose twice in the tournament" – a reference to the tying shot at the buzzer (it later appeared to be after the buzzer) which allowed the Yellow Jackets to beat Michigan State in overtime in an early-round matchup.

Meanwhile, Duke's "dynasty in search of a title" handled Arkansas easily, 97-83, in the other semifinal matchup, capping a consistent tournament performance after a sometimes shaky regular season. Coach Mike Krzyzewski's Blue Devils had made it to the Final Four for the third year in a row and fourth time in five years. Yet Duke, led by leading scorer Phil Henderson and fine sophomore forward Christian Laettner, was searching for a way to shake off its "always the bridesmaid, never the bride" reputation. This year, however, they were simply overmatched.

The championship game was a march of glory for UNLV's unofficial tourney "bad guys," and perhaps a disappointment to the casual NCAA fan who had become used to the heart-stopping finishes of the title games of the previous five years. It was UNLV's game all the way, even as most of the season had belonged to them – they had been voted number one in most preseason polls and had finished a wild and woolly season rated number two nationally.

A crowd of some 17,000 in Denver's McNichols Sports Arena (or "Big Mac," as some have nicknamed it) were treated to a basketball clinic – one which included demonstrations of the art of the fast break, the slam dunk and the steal. Rebel Larry Johnson hit three-point shots with regularity, and the UNLV team as a whole managed a near-record 61.2% shooting percentage from the field. Anderson Hunt of the Runnin' Rebels scored a game-high 29 points to garner MVP honors, while point guard Greg Anthony chipped in with 13 points, five steals and six assists.

Duke's Henderson scored 21 points in defeat, but managed only 1-for-8 from three-point range for a team that never seemed able to rally from UNLV's pounding offense. At one point, the Rebs engineered a three-minute, 18-straight-point blitz which seemed to take the wind out of Duke's sails. Henderson later said, "When we played better, so did they. It seemed like they never got tired. Maybe nobody told them that we're a mile high here, and they weren't supposed to do that." Coach Krzyzewski later said it was the best a team had ever played against him as a coach.

For Tarkanian, the win was perhaps a vindication of his embattled UNLV program, but more a treasure to be savored. "It wasn't revenge, but it was sweet," he later said. "Winning the trophy wasn't a personal thing with me. Nevada and Las Vegas get knocked a lot. I look at it as a big event for the people there."

Left: *Tourney MVP Anderson Hunt puts a victorious arm around his UNLV coach, Jerry Tarkanian, after the Runnin' Rebels won the 1990 NCAA title game.*

Right: *Duke's Alaa Abdelnaby goes up for a shot in early action during the title game against UNLV. The Rebels outplayed Duke for the 103-73 win.*

Far right: *It was UNLV's game all the way, as a defiant Rebel forward Moses Scurry demonstrates.*

35

(Numerals in italics indicate illustrations)